MARYLAND AND DELAWARE

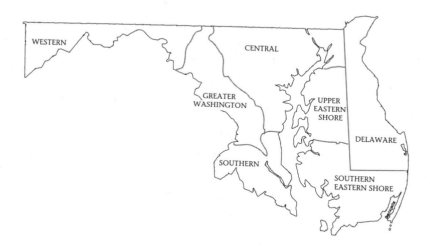

CONTENTS

INTRODUCTION

Welcome to the new *Maryland and Delaware: Off the Beaten Path.* You're about to explore two of the most fascinating places in this country. You're sure to find the best food, the most unusual attractions, the friendliest people, the most incredible history, the most amazing scenery, and the best way to spend a few hours off the interstate.

Maryland is known by several nicknames, including the Free State and America in Miniature; it also is known for its symbols. Delaware is called the First State and the Small Wonder. Together let us enjoy a sampling of all that these two states have to offer.

If you asked most Marylanders why they call it the Free State (road signs say KEEP THE FREE STATE LITTER FREE), they would probably cite the freedom of worship advocated by the state's founders. Others might point to Maryland's alliance with the northern states during "the war" and its intolerance of slavery. These historical facts are true, but the name dates from 1917, when the state opposed prohibition on the grounds that it was an issue to be decided by each state.

Maryland is America in Miniature primarily because of its diverse terrain, which stretches from the mountains to the seashore. The mountains are not high compared to the Rockies (Backbone Mountain in Garrett County is the tallest, at 3,360 feet), but they provide fair downhill and excellent cross-country skiing. The seashore is among the finest in the east.

Minute quantities of gold have been found along the Potomac, near Great Falls, and in the Piedmont regions. Stop by the Chesapeake and Ohio (C & O) Canal Park and Great Falls Tavern Museum, near the intersection of MacArthur Boulevard and Great Falls Road in Montgomery County. Park in the C & O Canal parking area and follow the unmarked trail to the Maryland Gold Mine, which was worked until the 1920s. No one has become rich on Maryland gold, but one can try. For more information about the history of gold finds in the state and rules and regulations about prospecting, write to the Maryland Geological Survey, 2300 St. Paul Street, Baltimore 21218.

Not everything in Maryland, however, is miniature. The National Aquarium in Baltimore is one of the world's largest. The

OFF THE BEATEN PATH™ SERIES

Maryland and Delaware

OFF THE BEATEN PATH™

THIRD EDITION

JUDY COLBERT

A Voyager Book

The Globe Pequot Press

Old Saybrook, Connecticut

Dedicated to Ben and Rockzana,
the newest travelers

Cover map copyright © DeLorme Mapping
Maps generated from originals by Ed Colbert and Judy Colbert
Art on page 119 by M. A. Dube; all other art by Carole Drong, rendered from photographs by Judy Colbert

Library of Congress Cataloging-in-Publication Data
Colbert, Judy.
    Maryland and Delaware : off the beaten path / Judy Colbert. — 3rd ed.
        p.   cm. -- (Off the beaten path series)
    "A Voyager book."
    Includes index.
    ISBN 1-56440-969-4
    1. Maryland and Delaware—Guidebooks. I. Title. II. Series.
F179.3.C65   1997
917.5204'43—dc20   96-38588
                                                                        CIP
Manufactured in the United States of America
Third Edition/Second Printing

collection at the Walters Art Gallery, also in Baltimore, is world renowned.

Maryland has many symbols. Maryland has a state tree (the Wye Oak), a state song ("Maryland, My Maryland" by James Ryder Randall), and a state crustacean (the blue crab). The state bird is the Baltimore oriole. If you cannot find it in the wild, check at Camden Yards.

The black-eyed Susan is the official flower, and you will see it blooming profusely by the side of the road and in wildflower beds from late spring through fall.

The state also has an official fossil, the four-ribbed snail, an extinct invertebrate that ranged in size from microscopic to 3 or 4½ inches in diameter. Fossils can be found at the Cliffs of Calvert, in the Choptank, and in the St. Mary's City area.

Go by the bay to watch the hunters at work, and frequently you will find Chesapeake Bay retrievers with them, for they are a native-bred amphibious hunter. There was a ban on catching striped bass or rockfish during the last four years of the 1980s, but that ban is now lifted, and there is not a better or sweeter-tasting fish than baked striped bass.

The state sport is jousting, the oldest equestrian sport in the world, with men and women competing. Like other sports and competitions, jousting originated as a test of man's occupational skills. In Maryland the challenge in jousting is not to toss a rider off his or her saddle, but to spear a series of metal rings while riding on a horse. The 80-yard course has three arches from which rings are suspended; in each round the size of the rings decreases. These are not huge rings to begin with; the largest ring is 1¾ inches in diameter and the smallest is ¼ inch.

There are numerous jousting tournaments throughout the year. The schedule usually starts in April and continues through to the Maryland State Championship and the Nationals in October. Events may take place in Hagerstown, Frederick, St. Mary's City, Easton, Denton, Trappe, Port Republic, Lily Pons, Clear Spring, Chestertown, and Havre de Grace. Each tournament has its pageantry and fun, its food and partying. Usually there is an admission charge, which often is used to benefit a charitable organization. Write to the Maryland Jousting Tournament Association, 328 Bush Chapel Road, Aberdeen 21001 for a schedule of events.

Note that as of 1997, Maryland will have two new area codes, in addition to the (301) and (410) codes. Generally (301) and (240) codes are for the western, suburban Maryland, and southern Maryland counties. Similarly (410) and (443) are for Annapolis, Baltimore, and Eastern Shore areas. In any case, beginning May 1, 1997, all local calls will require the entire ten-digit number (area code and phone number). Only long-distance calls require the number "1" before the ten-digit number.

The DelMarVa Peninsula (for *DEL*aware, *MAR*yland, and *Vir-giniA*) has always been that to me. I never once questioned whether it should have or at some other time might have been VaMarDel or MarVaDel or some other variation of the three states. Wade B. Fleetwood, who wrote a column about the people and places of the Eastern Shore, did question it, and now so have I. We have drawn no conclusion. It could be from north to south, or alphabetical, or political. I don't know. I do know that it was refered to as that as early as 1870, when the fourteen counties of the Eastern Shore (three in Delaware, nine in Maryland, and two in Virginia) were discussing separate statehood.

So, if the Delaware of DelMarVa comes first, why does this book list Maryland first? Because *Maryland: Off the Beaten Path* was here first, and it hasn't been until this third edition that it was expanded to include Delaware. Delaware is just too tiny to claim its own volume. I know someone out there is bound to say, "Well, all of Delaware is off the beaten path," and to a great extent that is deliciously true. Nancy Sawin, a famed Delaware illustrator, has caught the essence of the state and the peninsula in many of her books. The books are difficult to find, but they include a treasure of information about everything from outhouses to swamps to lighthouses.

This state of only three counties measures 110 miles long and 9 to 35 miles across. The Delaware Estuary is the major staging area for 80 percent of the snow geese in the Atlantic flyway. Delaware is also known as the state without sales tax, and there are a number of outlet stores and malls, particularly at Rehoboth Beach. (What else do you do besides shop on a rainy day during your vacation?)

Everywhere you turn in Delaware there's a delightful treasure, whether it's watching children get on a school bus, eyes and bodies filled with excitement and anticipation, or the changing song patterns of rain falling pitter-patter on the car roof, interrupted by the overhanging trees dropping huge glops of water. The scenic ponds created to supply energy to the dozens of gristmills and lumber mills are too perfect to be captured by mere artists or mere words. They have to be experienced firsthand. And the friendliness of everyone you meet is just too precious to appreciate in just one visit. You may have to move to Delaware and spend a lifetime in this Small Wonder and First State (to ratify the Constitution).

In researching and preparing this book, I avoided the most common attractions and sought the slightly offbeat, the friendly, the tasty, the visually perfect and imperfect, and the most creative sites. I hope you enjoy reading and using this book as much as I enjoyed discovering *Maryland and Delaware: Off the Beaten Path.*

The prices and rates listed in this guidebook were confirmed at press time. We recommend, however, that you call establishments before traveling to obtain current information.

WESTERN MARYLAND

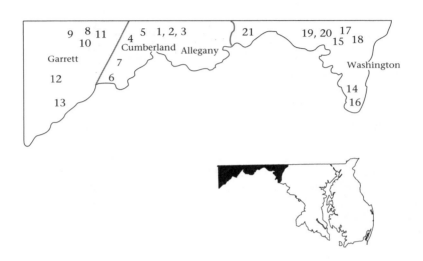

9 8 11 / 4 5 1, 2, 3   21   19, 20 17
   10   / Cumberland Allegany   15 18
Garrett   7   Washington
12   / 6   14
13   16

1. Constitution Park
2. Victorian Historic District
3. Western Maryland Scenic
   Railroad
4. Old Depot Center
5. Mt. Savage Castle
6. Westvaco Paper Company
7. Lonaconing Iron Furnace
8. Casselman Hotel
9. Casselman Bridge
10. Spruce Forest Artisan Village
11. Fuller–Baker Log House
12. Deep Creek Lake
13. Flying Scot, Inc. boat company

14. Valley Craft Network
15. Beaver Creek House Bed and
    Breakfast
16. Maple Tree Campground
17. Washington County Museum
    of Fine Art
18. Hagerstown Post Office
    murals
19. Wilson Village Old General
    Store
20. Historic Wilson Bridge Picnic
    Area
21. Sideling Hill

WESTERN MARYLAND

Western Maryland's three counties—Garrett, Allegany, and Washington—are a combination of farmlands, rugged mountains, sedate streams, and white-water rivers.

The products of farms and iron furnaces needed to be transported to customers between Wheeling, West Virginia, and the East Coast. So through this territory came the National Pike, which now is Alternate Route 40. It was the first road across the country funded by the federal government. This was long before President Eisenhower dictated there would be a national system of interstate highways. Along the road are many of the original mile markers, white metal (although they look like stone) obelisks that stand about 3 feet high. In LaVale (Allegany) you will find the only remaining tollhouse (circa 1836) in Maryland.

Paralleling the Potomac River to Cumberland was the Chesapeake and Ohio Canal. The canal was part of George Washington's dream of a water system that would unite the Atlantic with the Ohio River. The canal is now a National Historical Park. The 184½-mile towpath is used year-round by hikers, cyclists, and nature enthusiasts who enjoy seeing the restored aqueducts and canal locks and communing with nature.

Railroads superseded the canal as an efficient means of transportation. Today I–81, I–68, and I–70 provide the lifelines connecting this part of the state with the rest of the country.

The geographic features that isolated Western Maryland for so many years also made it attractive to vacationers; residents from Washington, D.C., and Baltimore traditionally have come here to escape the summer heat.

Here you will find traces of Amish and Scottish culture, of hardy stock and friendly people. You will note some wealth, both in property and in cultural heritage. As yet, you will not find hundreds of thousands of tourists. You will find hospitality, tranquillity, perseverance, a dedication to remember the "old ways," and beautiful mountain scenery.

ALLEGANY COUNTY

Outdoor enthusiasts enjoy Allegany County and Cumberland, the county seat. Within the county borders are Rocky Gap State

Park, Dan's Mountain, and Green Ridge State Forests, and the C & O Canal National Historical Park, where people can hunt, boat, fish, camp, and explore history.

Cumberland is considered the mibster capital of the country. For some reason the marble players of this town far surpass the players from other towns. A recent world champion was a twelve-year-old from Cumberland. If it has been a while since you played, or if you have never tried your hand at it, visit ◆ **Constitution Park.** In addition to the Little League baseball field, picnic groves, swimming pool, wading pool, playground, railroad caboose, 1937 fire truck, army tank, horseshoe pits, and courts for basketball, tennis, shuffleboard, volleyball, and badminton, there are two game areas with three marble rings each. Games and tournaments are held regularly at the park; six national marble champions have played and practiced here on their way to victory.

Constitution Park is off Williams Street in the southeast area of Cumberland. From Maryland Avenue turn left on Williams Street to reach the park entrance. Call (301) 759–6440.

A brochure is available to help you walk through the ◆ **Victorian Historic District** of Cumberland, beginning at the east bank of Will's Creek and extending to the western property line of 630 Washington Street. The brochure highlights the architectural details and historical importance of about three dozen buildings. One of these is the History House museum, which has eighteen rooms available for touring and features Victorian furniture, antiques, and displays pertaining to Allegany County's history.

There is also a brochure available on the Fort Cumberland Walking Trail, which highlights the site of the 1755 fort with plaques on its history. The trail passes by George Washington's headquarters, a cabin that he used when he served at the fort as an aide to General Edward Braddock during the French and Indian War. Another brochure, this one entitled "Walking Tour of Historic Downtown Cumberland," highlights the architectural gems in the Downtown Pedestrian Mall area.

The Western Maryland Station Center, which was in service from 1913 until 1976, is now a museum dedicated to the history of transportation and industry in Allegany County. The center also houses the Allegany County Visitor's Bureau, the Allegany Arts Council and Gallery, the Western Maryland Scenic Railroad, and the C & O Canal National Historical Park Visitor's Center. Exhibits in the museum highlight the railroad, the National Pike (the first federal toll highway constructed across the country), the C & O Canal (a full-size lock is included in the exhibits), and such local industries as brewing and distilling, iron making, glassmaking, tire making (Kelly-Springfield), and mining. Mercantile establishments and the local First and Last Chance Saloon are represented as well.

The Allegany Arts Council has twenty-four arts organizations actively involved in choral singing, theater, cinema, photography, crafts, instrumental music, and visual arts. Classes are scheduled regularly, and a gallery exhibits works that are for sale. The Canal Visitor's Center has an interpretive display in the station, where photographs, models, and artifacts are exhibited.

The Industrial and Transportation Museum is open Tuesday through Sunday from 10:00 A.M. to noon and 2:00 to 4:00 P.M. The Allegany Arts Council and Gallery is open Monday through Friday from 9:00 A.M. to 3:00 P.M. and the telephone is (301) 777–2787. The C & O Canal National Historical Park Visitor's Center is open Tuesday from 11:00 A.M. to 4:00 P.M., Wednesday through Saturday 10:00 A.M. to 5:00 P.M., and Sunday 1:00 to 4:00 P.M. The Allegany County Visitor's Bureau is open May through October 9:00 A.M. to 5:00 P.M. daily and November through April 9:00 A.M. to 8:00 P.M. Monday through Friday and 10:00 A.M. to 4:00 P.M. on weekends. Call (301) 777–5905.

The romance of early twentieth-century steam railroading is with us once more on the ❖ **Western Maryland Scenic Railroad,** where passengers take a 17-mile ride combining mountaintop scenery and rich transportation history. The Western Maryland features a locomotive built in 1916 by the Baldwin Locomotive Works for the Lake Superior & Ishpeming Railroad, based in Michigan. It is a Consolidation 2–8–0 used from 1916 to 1956 for switching and freight hauling in Michigan's Upper Peninsula. It was on display at the Illinois Railroad Museum from 1971 until it was purchased by the WMSR in 1992.

As the train steams its way up the 2.8 percent grade on the westward trip from Cumberland to Frostburg, it travels along old Western Maryland Railway and Cumberland and Pennsylvania Railway rights-of-way. Riders view many memorable sights, including the

4

famous Cumberland Narrows (a natural 1,000-foot breach in Will's Mountain known as the "Gateway to the West"), an iron truss bridge, Bone Cave, and Helmstetter's Horseshoe Curve. Other interesting sights along the way include the 1,000-foot Brush Mountain Tunnel, the Allegheny Front, Victorian architecture, the C & O Canal, Buck's Horse Farm, and the frontier town of Mt. Savage (where America's first iron rails were produced). At the Frostburg terminus you can get a close-up view of the engineer and fireman in blue-and-white overalls and the locomotive turntable, which reverses the engine for the return journey.

At the other end, in Frostburg, James Oberhaus, Jr., has restored the ◆ **Old Depot Center** complex, which now features a restaurant, an ice-cream parlor, a bakery, and the Thrasher Carriage Collection. This collection offers more than fifty examples of early nineteenth- and twentieth-century horse-drawn vehicles. Built by the finest manufacturers, the vehicles include a Vanderbilt family sleigh and the formal coach used by Theodore Roosevelt at his inauguration. Call (301) 589–3380 or 777–5905.

Also take time to wander through the craft and souvenir shops located in the restored Tunnel Hotel, or visit the quaint shops and restaurants along the main street of Frostburg, just a few blocks away.

The rail trip takes about three hours, including a ninety-minute layover in Frostburg. A special dining car has been dedicated as the Governor William Donald Schaefer Special for the governor who was credited with inspiring state, local, and private development of the scenic railroad.

The train runs weekends only in April, November, and December and Tuesday through Sunday from May through October. There's an expanded schedule in October for fall foliage viewing. Ticket prices are $14.75 for adults, $13.25 for seniors, and $9.50 for children ages 2 to 12. Prices may vary in October.

Charter trips and special events such as dinner trips or trips featuring murder mysteries, dinner theater, or dancing are scheduled periodically. Private parties for weddings, birthdays, business meetings, school outings, and other events also may be booked. Write to Western Maryland Scenic Railroad, Western Maryland Station, Canal Street, Cumberland 21502, or call (800)

TRAIN–50 or (301) 759–4400. Visit the WMSR on the Internet at http://www.wmsr.com.

One of the sights you will see on the railroad excursion, or on a drive through Mt. Savage, is the ◆ **Mt. Savage Castle.** This National Historic Landmark in stone, built in 1874, is a replica of the Craig Castle in Scotland. At the height of its grandeur, the castle was owned by industrialist Andrew Ramsay, a Scot who was renowned for his production of ceramic glazed brick, which can be found throughout the building. He also planted the rare trees and abundant flowers that overflow the estate.

The castle's twenty-eight rooms, nine bathrooms, carriage house, and terraced gardens have been restored to their former elegance and furnished with antiques by William and Andrea Myer. Bob and Lisa Miller now own and operate the castle as a bed and breakfast with six elegantly furnished sleeping rooms. Four rooms have private baths; two rooms share a large main bathroom. A full breakfast is provided for overnight guests, and high tea is served at 4:00 P.M. Weather permitting, both are served in the outside courtyard or porticoes. In keeping with the Scottish tradition, croquet and putting can be enjoyed on the grassed terrace. Tours, receptions, parties, conferences, and other special events may be booked at the castle. Privacy is assured by the 20-foot stone wall that surrounds the grounds. The address is 15925 Mt. Savage Road, The Castle, Mt. Savage 21545. Call (301) 759–5946.

Just as the railroad and the canal played an important part in the area's development, the National Pike has a claim to fame. You can drive to the top of either side of the Cumberland Narrows for an unparalleled view, on a clear day, of Cumberland and the surrounding countryside. To reach the eastern wall of the Narrows, take Will's Mountain Road off Piedmont Avenue to the parking lot of Artmor Plastics, park, and walk about 2 blocks. To reach the western wall, take exit 41, the Sacred Heart Hospital exit, off I–68. Go through the traffic light and up the hill to Bishop Walsh Road, where you will turn right to the high school. Drive to the back of the school, where the road ends, and walk through the woods, past the water tower, to the edge—about a five-minute walk. This is not a prepared path and it is not handicapped accessible.

Mt. Savage Castle

◆**Westvaco Paper Company** at Luke spreads over three counties and two states—Allegany and Garrett in Maryland and Mineral in West Virginia. The town is named for William Luke, who founded the paper company on this site in 1888. The company manufactures more than 1,200 tons of high-quality, coated, white printing papers each day. The products are used for such magazines as *Forbes, Town & Country, Good Housekeeping, Fortune,* and Disney and National Geographic Society publications.

A ninety-minute tour allows visitors to view the papermaking process from pulpwood to cooking to the finished rolls and sheets. Call (301) 359–3311 to arrange a tour. The company prefers about two weeks' notice.

When you are driving from the Oakland area of Garrett County to Luke, you will have several miles of a very steep downhill grade on Route 135 where trucks are cautioned to drive no more than 10 miles an hour. If you are caught behind one of these trucks, slip into low gear (in the car and in your mind) and spend a little time looking at the beautiful countryside—something you would not be able to do if you were rushing through at 55 miles an hour. That is why you are off the beaten path, isn't it?

The ◆**Lonaconing Iron Furnace** was erected about 1836 by the George's Creek Coal and Iron Company and produced iron for the next twenty years. When the furnace was constructed, it was unique in several respects. It was 50 feet high and 50 feet square at the base—a daring departure from contemporary furnaces, which were 30 feet high and 30 feet square. Moreover, it was the first furnace built in this country that successfully used coke fuel at a time when all furnaces were using the less efficient charcoal.

The furnace was built against a hillside because it was fed from the top. The site was chosen because the necessary iron ore, coal, wood, clay, limestone, sandstone, and water were readily available, although transportation to the marketplace was not convenient. Castings made here included stoves, farming implements, and dowels for the C & O Canal lock walls.

Today the furnace is the backdrop for a pleasant town park in Lonaconing, where you can stop to lunch at the picnic tables or enjoy the play equipment. A sign notes the location of the former Central School, and a bronze plaque honors Robert Moses

Lonaconing Iron Furnace

"Lefty" Grove, a native son who was elected into the Baseball Hall of Fame in 1947. Lauded as the greatest left-handed pitcher of all time, he played for the Philadelphia Athletics from 1925 to 1933 and the Boston Braves from 1934 to 1941. The furnace is located on Route 36, Main Street, in Lonaconing.

For additional information, write to Natalie K. Chabot, Manager, Allegany County Visitor's Bureau, Mechanic and Harrison Streets, Cumberland 21502, or call (301) 777–5905 or (800) 508–4748.

GARRETT COUNTY

Garrett County claims several Maryland honors. It is the county farthest west, and it has the highest mountain (Backbone, at 3,360 feet), the longest waterfall (Muddy Creek Falls, at 52 feet), and the largest lake (Deep Creek, with a length of 12 miles and a 65-mile shoreline).

Reportedly it also has the only town in the country named Accident. The story is that George Deakins was given a land grant for 600 acres in western Maryland in 1751 by King George II. Deakins sent two engineers on separate missions to find his paradise. By accident, each selected the same plot starting at the same tall oak tree. Deakins called this plot "The Accident Tract," and the name endures; locals wouldn't have it any other way. Most noted by visitors are the Accident Garage, the Accident Fire Department, and the Accident Professional Building.

The **Drane House,** built in the late eighteenth century, just east of Accident, is one of the few original frontier plantation homes remaining in this area. A key to Accident's past, it has been restored and is open for free tours upon request. Call the Accident Town Hall, Monday, Wednesday, and Friday, at (301) 746–6346.

Another historic small town is **McHenry,** permanently settled about 1805 by Colonel James McHenry, aide to General George Washington, signer of the Declaration of Independence, and the man for whom the Baltimore fort was named.

Vacationers have been seeking respite in Garrett County for hundreds of years, and traces of that history can be found throughout the county. The Shawnee Indians summered here. People from the sun-baked, humid cities of Washington and Baltimore came here to enjoy the cool mountain climate as early as 1851. That is when the Baltimore and Ohio Railroad ran its line to Oakland, which would become the county seat. The train no longer stops in Garrett County, but the Oakland station, an outstanding and picturesque Queen Anne structure built in 1884, remains.

The **Oakland Post Office Mural** was created by Robert Gates in 1942; it portrays a buckwheat harvest. Gates also did the mural in the Bethesda Post Office, which depicts the Montgomery County Farm Woman's Cooperative Market.

Presidents Ulysses S. Grant, William Henry Harrison, and Grover Cleveland enjoyed this area as their vacation spot, and William McKinley stopped here while campaigning for office. Thomas Edison, Henry Ford, and Harvey Firestone camped by Muddy Creek Falls in 1918 and again in 1921. Even Albert Einstein is said to have spent two weeks here in 1946.

Grover Cleveland and his bride, Frances Folsom, stayed in the three-story, fourteen-room "Cottage Number Two," now "Cleveland Cottage," near the **Deer Park Hotel** for their fifteen-day wedding trip in 1886. The Deer Park Hotel was built in 1873 by the Baltimore and Ohio Railroad when John W. Garrett (for whom the county was named) was company president. None of the hotel's main structure remains because it was razed in 1942, but some of the foundation is still visible. About 5 miles east of Oakland, on Route 135, turn south on Deer Park Hotel Road and proceed ½ mile, then drive east on the loop at Pennington Cottage to reach the hotel.

Solomon Sterner opened the ◆**Casselman Hotel** in Grantsville in 1824 to take in travelers from the National Pike. As is usual with restaurants, inns, and hotels along the pike, this one is on the north side, or the side that westbound travelers would be on.

When the nearby ◆**Casselman Bridge** was built in 1813, it was the largest single-span, stone-arch bridge in America. Gracefully curving 50 feet above the river, it was constructed so that the Chesapeake and Ohio Canal could travel beneath its span. The canal never came this far, but the bridge carried traffic for 125 years. It is now closed to motorized traffic, but there's a picnic area and a scenic spot to enjoy for a few minutes or a few hours.

East of Casselman Bridge is Penn Alps, home to numerous crafters who work in log cabins that have been brought here from the surrounding countryside. The shops in ◆**Spruce Forest Artisan Village** are open from late May through late October. One of the better-known artists is Grantsville native and resident Gary Yoder. Yoder is a renowned bird carver who uses his chisels, knives, wood burners, and other tools to create birds that win prizes in international competition. In September 1989 Yoder won a $20,000 prize for his robins at the Ward Foundation world championships in Ocean City, Maryland, and he continues his award-winning ways.

Yoder has been carving since he was eleven, and his carvings can command from $300 to more than $10,000. Orders can take from two to four years to fill. When you visit Yoder's bird-carving cabin, he will be delighted to explain how he carves the birds. He may test your visual acuity by asking you to distinguish between his carved bird feather and a real bird feather. Other crafts are sold in the gift shop.

Penn Alps is on Route 40 in Grantsville. The Artisan Village phone number is (301) 895–3332.

Garrett County has drawn even more artistic talent with the relocation of Mark and Laura Stutzman, who operate Eloqui illustration studio. You've seen Mark's work on numerous McDonald's packages (Batman, Jurassic Park), but he's best known for designing the Elvis Presley postage stamp for the "Legends in American Music" series. Look for activities sponsored by the Garrett Lakes Arts Festival, and you'll probably find both Mark and Laura in attendance.

About a mile east of Grantsville, still on the National Pike, is the ◆**Fuller-Baker Log House.** The house is representative of those constructed on the Allegheny frontier, except that it is large enough to have been a tavern. It is believed to be the only remaining log tavern on the National Pike between Cumberland and Wheeling. Maryland's first governor, Thomas Johnson, owned the property when the house was built in 1815, but it is named for two other longtime residents. The first was Henry Fuller, who came to the area in 1837 to work as a stonemason. The Bakers were also early settlers and owned the house at a later date. The house in now on the National Register of Historic Places.

Woodcarver Dennis Ruane is restoring the log tavern for use as a studio. Ruane was one of the demonstrators at Penn Alps after he moved here in 1984; today you can see his work, which is a mix of large and small items, such as spoons and Christmas tree ornaments, when you stop by the log house. Contact Ruane at P.O. Route 1, Grantsville 21536, or call (301) 895–3172.

In 1925, a dam 1,300 feet long and 62 feet high was constructed to provide hydroelectric power, and ◆ **Deep Creek Lake** resulted. It is fed by Deep and Cherry creeks, seven stream runs, and two glades. Rafters on the Upper Youghiogheny River (or Upper Yough, pronounced "yock") fight their way over Gap and Bastard falls and through rapids with names like Charlie's Choice, Rocky III, Cheeseburger, and Meat Cleaver.

In the 9-mile ride there are twenty Class IV and V rapids (the top of the scale being class VI) and a downhill drop of 100 to 120 feet per mile. These rapids can provide some tough but exhilarating times; an experienced guide is a necessity.

When the Whitewater Canoe/Kayak World Championships were held in the United States for the first time in 1989, they were held on nearby Savage River, another popular rafting place. Then, in 1992, the river was the site of the canoe and kayak team Olympic trials.

Other recreational pastimes in Garrett County include water sports, skiing (downhill and cross country), hiking, camping, golfing, horseback riding, hunting, and mountain biking. The mountains in this area receive the second-largest annual snowfall in the East (after the White Mountains of New Hampshire), which makes for good downhill skiing at Wisp (Deep Creek Lake) and extraordinary cross-country skiing.

Within the more than 70,000 acres of public land, Garrett County has cleared and marked trails in **Germany State Park,** 6 miles of maintained trails around Herrington Lake, and an additional 6 miles of primitive trails. Deep Creek and Swallow Falls State Parks have marked hiking trails that are suitable for cross-country skiing. Ski rentals are available at Herrington Manor and New Germany State Park.

The climate, people, and recreational offerings in the area combined to attract Gordon K. "Sandy" Douglas about thirty years ago, when he started building his Flying Scot sailboat at the ◆ **Flying Scot, Inc., boat company.** Today Harry and Karen Carpenter own and operate the company, overseeing the construction of these handmade boats, which come out of the plant at the rate of about two a week.

The Carpenters have maintained the image and reputation of the hugely popular Flying Scot. This fast 19-footer has a wide beam and a large center cockpit. It also features a fiberglass centerboard instead of a keel. It can be sailed by one, but it will carry eight people comfortably on a day's sail. A novice supposedly can learn the basics in six hours. Lessons are available from Deep Creek Sailing School. Call (301) 387–4497.

If you like to look at sailboats, you can tour the plant at Deer Park. Call (301) 334–4848.

About 20 miles east of Oakland is the Baltimore and Ohio Viaduct at Bloomington. It was opened in 1851 to connect the port of Baltimore with industrial Wheeling and the Ohio Valley. The multispan, stone-and-concrete bridge carries the railroad across the North Branch of the Potomac River. A Confederate raiding party schemed to demolish the viaduct but was driven away by Union troops before the bridge could be blasted. Blasting holes drilled by Captain John H. McNeill and his McNeill's Rangers are still visible on the bridge. The Baltimore and Ohio Viaduct is on Route 135, just west of the Garrett and Allegany county line.

Garrett has one other "first" honor. In 1989 Frank "Doc" Custer sent 3,200 of his white pine and balsam fir Christmas trees to the Bahamas. This was the first time that a Maryland grower had exported trees outside the United States. Custer planted his first tree in 1956, and his Mountain Top Tree Farm, outside Oakland, is one of the largest tree farms in the state. As you drive around the county and spot perfect trees for your next holiday season, remember it may be going to Nassau to brighten up the holidays for someone who misses snow and cold weather.

For additional information contact Deep Creek Lake–Garrett County Promotion Council, 200 South Third Street, Oakland 21550, or call (301) 334–1948. The e-mail address is G-C Tourism @ gcc.cc.md.us.

WASHINGTON COUNTY

Washington County—the first county to be named after George Washington—was founded on September 6, 1776, just months

14

after our country itself was born. In a Civil War battle fought at Sharpsburg, along Antietam Creek, more than 23,000 casualties were suffered.

Since 1989 an annual remembrance of the battle has been held the first Saturday in December; it is signified by 23,100 luminaries placed every 10 feet along 4½ miles of roadway, in the fields, along Bloody Lane, and around some of the monuments erected on the battlefield. It takes 400 volunteers to set the lights, starting at 3:30 P.M. About 3,000 cars drive through to look at the candles, starting about 5:30 P.M.; the candles burn about ten hours. The luminaries are paid for by corporate sponsors, and the drive is free, but a donation is requested.

The idea for the candles came from the Rest Haven cemetery, which had previously placed a luminary at every grave site. Borrowing the idea, Hagerstown residents lit luminaries every night for the two weeks prior to Christmas. One night it was the north side of town, another it was the south side, and so it continued throughout the area. Band members of the high schools sold 81,000 lights in the neighborhoods.

The newest monument, the first to be erected since 1967 and probably the last ever, is scheduled to be installed on September 17, 1997. This is a tribute to the **Irish Brigade** that fought on Bloody Lane. More than 500 men were slaughtered or wounded in this battle, but they have never been formally recognized. The campaign to have this monument erected helped cause the creation of the Adopt-a-Monument National Battlefield program.

Budget cuts have reduced the funding of preservation and rehabilitation programs for the 103 monuments, and more than half of them have major sculptural elements, statues, carved reliefs, and ornamental embellishments. Now people and groups can donate time, supplies, or money to support the park or a specific monument or marker. Contributions, small enough to buy a paintbrush or large enough to paint, repair, and seal a War Department tablet for about $250, are readily accepted.

Jane Kemble handles the Adopt-a-Monument program and can be reached at P.O. Box 158, Sharpsburg 21782; (301) 432–7648.

Washington County parks rate with the best and include the C & O Canal National Historical Park, the Appalachian Trail (37 miles), Fort Frederick State Park, Washington Monument State

Park, Pen Mar County Park (and at least eight other county parks), and Hagerstown City Park. **Hagerstown,** the county seat of Washington County, is also the home of the *Hagers-Town Town and Country Almanack,* which has been printed since 1797. The weather forecasts generate the most interest, and people swear by them. In fact, a folk tale has it that the book called for snow on July 4, 1874, and that it did snow on that date. Research indicates that the almanac did not predict snow, and the minimum temperature for that day was said to have been in the high sixties—not too conducive to snow.

You might wonder, without being arrogant, how people live so far out in the country. You think about snow blocking roads for days and people being miles from a store or a neighbor. Where do these people work? What do they do for a living?

One set of answers can be found in the members of the ◆ **Valley Craft Network.** This group of nine artisans (which changes periodically as members leave or join the network), most of whom are in Washington County, spend their days creating works of art and their weekends traveling around the countryside visiting craft shows. Twice a year, in late April and on the first weekend in December, they sponsor a **Studio Tour.** Many people make a weekend visit out of this tour.

A map and STUDIO TOUR signs help you negotiate the back roads of Pleasant Valley between Hagerstown, Frederick, and Harper's Ferry, so you completely forget you're barely an hour from Washington or Baltimore. A side benefit of the winter tour is that every studio has a steaming pot of apple cider and something to nibble on to warm you up on a nippy day.

Each crafter has a catalog or some type of brochure from which you can order. You can visit most of the artisans any time of the year, with the normal precaution of calling ahead to make sure someone will be there. There are many other crafters throughout the valley who are worthy of your attention besides the members of the Valley Craft Network. Advertising signs along the roadway or brochures in shops let you know where they are. The following list includes only network members and provides just a sampling of the many local crafts you can enjoy.

Bill and Victoria Van Gilder of Van Gilder Potttery make functional pottery by hand in colonial blues and teal greens. The pottery is located at the entrance to Gathland State Park on South

Mountain at Gapland and is open Tuesday through Saturday from 10:00 A.M. to 5:00 P.M. Call (301) 416–2970.

At Ziem Vineyards Bob and Ruth Ziem produce award-winning, estate-bottled wines with an emphasis on quality that can be found only in smaller wineries. Tours and tastings are available. Located at 16651 Spielman Road, Fairplay 21733, the vineyards are open Thursday through Sunday 1:00 to 6:00 P.M. Call (301) 223–8352.

Minutes away is Foxcross Pottery, where Del Martin is known for his wheel-thrown tableware, lamps, sinks, and planters. You'll find him at Remsburg Road, Sharpsburg 21782. The pottery is open Saturday and Sunday from 10:00 A.M. to 5:00 P.M. Call (301) 432–6692.

For fine furniture and accessories made utilizing traditional joinery techniques in American hardwoods, call Michael and Louise Harris at Harris Furniture Company. Open by appointment, it's located at 2514 Poffenberger Road, Middletown 21769. Call (301) 371–4977.

Michelle Reilly produces traditional quilts, contemporary woven clothing, and handspun yarns in brilliant colors for sale at Wool 'n' Quilts. Her products all begin with the lambs and sheep on her farm. Open by appointment, the shop is at 4614 Locust Grove Road, Rohrersville 21779. Call (301) 432–2009.

Eric Madsen creates functional stoneware in a restored barn at Chance Regained Farm. Call Eric Madsen Pottery at (301) 432–2874 to schedule an appointment. The barn is at 20533 Park Hall Road, Rohrersville 21779.

Nancy Walz creates herbal and everlasting wreaths and bouquets at Surreybrooke. She also sells hand-dipped candles in her restored summer kitchen at 8537 Hollow Road, Middletown 21769. Her shop is open Wednesday through Saturday from 10:00 A.M. to 5:00 P.M. and Sunday from 1:00 to 5:00 P.M. Call (301) 371–7466.

At Catoctin Pottery Susan Hanson produces stoneware, dinnerware sets, wall art, lamps, in a wide variety of glazing patterns. The pottery is located in a restored 1820 gristmill, off Old Middletown Road, Jefferson 21755, and it's open Monday through Saturday from 10:00 A.M. to 5:00 P.M. Call (301) 731–4274.

Jan Richardson with her Window Meadows Pottery, is perhaps the best-known crafter in the valley; her hand-built stoneware houses can be seen everywhere. From a little privy (a night-light for your modern privy) to a chapel, from a train depot to an ice-cream parlor, you can find the perfect representation of yesterday's small town. Some items are created in limited editions and have become valued collector's items.

If you travel at times other than the Studio Tour, you can visit the Windy Meadows operation to see how clay is readied for the various artisans who hand-assemble them in their homes. Periodically, Jan issues a newsletter and photo brochure, which includes her schedule of craft shows. Windy Meadows Pottery is located at 1036 Valley Road, Knoxville 21758. Call (800) 527–6274; it's open Monday through Friday from 10:00 A.M. to 3:00 P.M.

While you are at any of the studios, you can ask for a list of nearby restaurants and other attractions.

A favorite of mine is the ✤**Beaver Creek House Bed and Breakfast,** operated by Don and Shirley Day. The house was built in 1905 and the rooms are filled with family antiques and memorabilia. The white-brick home with dark shutters is huge, yet warm and friendly with a great wraparound porch where you can sit on a swing and watch the scenery go by. Particularly pleasing are sunrises over the Blue Ridge Mountains, should you be up that early. Guests in any of the seven rooms may have breakfast on the screened porch, in the courtyard, or in the dining room and share afternoon tea in the parlor.

The bed and breakfast is located at 20432 Beaver Creek Road, Hagerstown 21740. Call (301) 797–4764.

For lodgings with a real twist, you'll want to visit ✤**Maple Tree Campground** near Gathland State Park. The unusual feature of this campground is that you sleep in a tree house. Did you always want one when you were a kid, but you lived in the city, or the only adults around had sixteen thumbs? This is not quite as rustic as you might remember, but it is as close as most of us will ever get. Your tree house—on stilts about 7 feet off the ground—has a couple of bunks (bring a sleeping bag), a wood stove, a table with benches, and a filled woodbin. A communal bathhouse is nearby, you have twenty-six acres of woods to roam through and explore, and you're not far from the Appalachian Trail. You may bring your tent for "regular" camping.

When Phyllis Sorocko started this campground after retirement, she dreaded the idea of tearing up the land and trees for campsites and dumpsites and was thrilled with this compromise. Pets, on leash at all times, are welcome. Reservations are recommended. The campground is located on Townsend Road, Gapland 21736. Call (301) 432–5585.

The ✦ **Washington County Museum of Fine Art** is an outstanding museum overlooking the fifty-acre City Park Lake (home to numerous waterfowl). It was the idea and gift of Mr. and Mrs. William Henry Singer, Jr., who had collected many possessions during their European travels and were looking for a beautiful place to house them. The cornerstone was laid on July 15, 1930, by Mrs. Singer's grandniece, Anna Spencer Brugh.

The museum was built of homewood brick with Indiana limestone trim. Two wings were added in 1949: the Memorial Gallery, in honor of Mr. Singer, who died in 1943, and the Concert Gallery, in honor of Mrs. Singer's love of music. Mrs. Singer was eighty-six when she died in Laren, Holland, in 1962.

Among the museum's collection are the works of Mr. Singer, who was a postimpressionist painter of note. Many of his landscapes show the fishing villages, fjords, and snow-covered mountains of Norway, where the Singers lived. Also in the collection are old masters, twentieth-century sculpture and painting, and a variety of decorative arts from around the world. The emphasis, though, is on American art.

In addition to tours, the museum offers art classes (weaving, clay, acrylics, quilting, and more), lectures, films, and music recitals. A bimonthly calendar is available.

The museum, located on City Park Lake, is open Tuesday through Saturday from 10:00 A.M. to 5:00 P.M. and Sunday from 1:00 to 6:00 P.M. A donation is requested. Call (301) 739–5727.

Three ✦ **Hagerstown Post Office murals** represent different aspects of the railway transportation of mail. The paintings were done by Frank Long of Berea, Kentucky, in 1938 as part of the Section of Fine Arts program—placing appropriate art in federal buildings. The first painting depicts mailbags being loaded onto a train. A central panel depicts a railway post office in operation, with postal clerks sorting letters on a train. The third panel, over the lockboxes, shows figures on the station platform watching an approaching train that will pick up the mail. Frank Long also painted post office murals in Louisville and Berea, Kentucky; Crawfordsville, Indiana; and Drumright, Oklahoma.

Boonsboro is known for its Civil War museum, but those who

19

Wilson Village Old General Store

really know it, know to visit in August and September when Boonsboro cantaloupes ripen. You can buy them from a roadside stand, particularly on Saturdays and Sundays, but it's best to plan an outing and pick your own. Then you'll really enjoy the thin-skinned, "Heart of Gold" variety with all its natural sweetness. The ✪ **Wilson Village Old General Store** is a classic country store with a post office, penny candy, yard goods, and much more. You'll also see a one-room schoolhouse. The store is on Old Route 40, and it is open daily. Call (301) 582–4718.

On your way to Wilson Village from Hagerstown, you may stop by the ✪ **Historic Wilson Bridge Picnic Area.** It's located along Route 40 West, adjacent to Historic Wilson Bridge, which is the oldest, longest, and most graceful of twenty-three stone-arch bridges in the county. The five-arch span was built in 1819 as an early extension of the National Pike to the Ohio Valley. The structure was erected by Pennsylvanian Silas Harry at a cost of $12,000. Its style represented a triumph for the justices of the Levy Court (until 1829, the body similar to a Board of County Commissioners) who insisted on an all-stone structure in the face of army engineers' arguments that a wooden bridge laid over stone piers would suffice.

The bridge is about 200 feet north of the west end of the "new" bridge crossing Conococheague Creek, 5 miles west of Hagerstown on Route 40. This one-acre site offers picnic tables, parking, and canoe access to the Conococheague.

Of particular interest to sports fans is the **Hagerstown Suns** baseball team of the South Atlantic League. This A team draws more than 160,000 fans a year; it is a farm club of the Toronto Blue Jays. In previous years, loyalists have seen the likes of Jeff Ballard, Jim Palmer, Bill Ripken, and Craig Worthington, all of whom have gone on to be well known in the baseball world. Palmer was elected to the Baseball Hall of Fame in 1989, his first year of eligibility. For information call the Municipal Stadium at (301) 791–6266.

The Washington County tourism office has a number of interesting brochures, and the personnel there are delighted to help you. Those traveling with children, or those who are young at heart, will like visiting Crystal Grottoes caverns or going on the ghost walk at Fort Frederick at Halloween time.

Seven miles west of Hancock, near the border between Allegany and Washington counties is ◆ **Sideling Hill.** A new freeway, officially designated I–68, diverts traffic off a steep, tricky road that twists to a roundhouse curve at the top of Sideling Hill. The 4½–mile section of the road took twenty-eight months to complete and cost about $21 million. Workers blasted an incredible, breathtaking 360-foot-deep cut in the mountain, which revealed millions of years of geological history; all this to achieve a relatively flat roadway. A three-and-a-half–story, handicapped-accessible interpretive center, which is approachable from both sides of the highway, will let you see all those layers and folds of multihued rocks that have been exposed by the cut and will explain their geologic history.

If you can make only one side trip in Maryland, only a momentary detour, this is the one to make. A late fall visit just may bring a surprise of a southern migration of ladybugs. In 1994 and 1995 there were so many millions of these critters that they obscured the windows and just about any other surface on which they could land. They've always migrated this way, but never before in these numbers. The sight is truly amazing. For information about Sideling Hill, call Fort Frederick State Park at (301) 842-2155.

For additional tourism information, write to Leroy Burtner, Washington County C&VB, 16 Public Square, Hagerstown 21740; (301) 791–3246 or (800) 228–7829.

CENTRAL MARYLAND

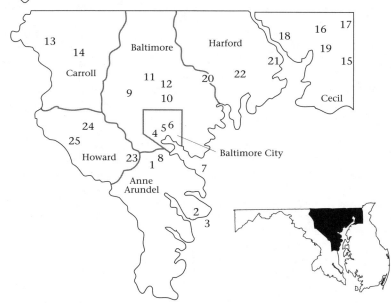

1. Baltimore–Washington International Airport (BWI)
2. Banneker–Douglass Museum
3. U.S. Naval Academy Museum
4. Top of the World observation deck and museum
5. Maryland Vietnam Veterans Memorial
6. Painted screens
7. General Motors Baltimore Assembly Plant
8. Calvert Distilling Company
9. Wild Acres Trail
10. Asian Arts Center
11. Oregon Ridge Park and Nature Center
12. Ashland Furnace
13. Bicycle tours
14. Ghosts of Carroll County
15. Little Wedding Chapel
16. Covered bridges
17. Fair Hill Inn
18. Conowingo Hydroelectric Plant
19. Day Basket Factory
20. Jericho Covered Bridge
21. Susquehanna Trading Company
22. Liriodendron
23. Thomas Viaduct
24. Cider Mill Farm and Larriland Farms
25. Toby's the Dinner Theatre of Columbia

CENTRAL MARYLAND

Perhaps nowhere in the state is there more diversity than in the area referred to as Central Maryland. In the rolling foothills and picturesque landscapes of this region are horse farms and vineyards, the commercial center of Baltimore city, huge stone farmhouses and old mills, busy waterways surrounding the Chesapeake Bay and its tributaries, some of the oldest towns in the country, and modern, vibrant cities. This core of six counties and two major cities encompasses it all.

This is the area that almost every travel writer writes about. In keeping with the "off the beaten path" dictum, I have looked for the unusual even in that which is familiar.

Sixteen million vehicles use the William Preston Lane, Jr., or Chesapeake Bay Bridge every year. Only 50,000 people walk across it, though, on Chesapeake Bay Bridge Walk Day. Once Maryland was a leading contender in the number of "kissing" or covered bridges; now there are only a few. See also Frederick and Prince George's counties in the Greater Washington section for more bridges.

Countless people stop by Annapolis to see its waterfront, Ego Alley (where the expensive boats parade), and the United States Naval Academy. They watch the sailboats in the harbor—even in the winter, when there is a Frostbite series of sailboat races—or the Naval Academy's noon meal formation, when the brigade of midshipmen assembles in front of Bancroft Hall for inspection. I chatted with Robert F. Sumrall, who re-creates scale models of the ships that have plied the bay.

Whenever anyone talks about Chesapeake Bay, blue crabs and oysters are sure to be discussed. I include a distinguished delicatessen, a bakery, an admirable place for ribs, a German restaurant that can compare with many fine art galleries, an old inn that is relatively new, and a scenic waterside eatery for sightseeing while you dine.

In a city as vibrant as Baltimore ("If you haven't seen Baltimore in five years, then you haven't seen Baltimore"), I chose to focus on the traditional: white marble steps and window screen painters.

I want you to do all the "touristy" things—spend an evening at the Morris Mechanic Theatre at Hopkins Plaza, eat crabs until you are elbow-deep in shells and seasonings at Harborplace, catch the superlative Walters Art Gallery—but I hope you will take time to visit some of my favorite "off the beaten path" places, too.

ANNE ARUNDEL COUNTY

Millions of people pass through ◆ **Baltimore-Washington International Airport (BWI)** to catch a plane, to pick up a passenger, or to go home. They do not realize that the airport has more to offer them for BWI has become a destination in itself. There's a beautiful observation gallery with information about flying and pieces of airplanes on display. There's also a cafe, a Smithsonian Shop, and nearby is the Market Walk with several gift shops.

BWI is one of the first major East Coast airports to establish a Web site for services and information and regional tourism information and offer links to airline and other travel service Web sites. The Web site has a terminal location map and travel tips. The BWI Web site is http://baltwashintlairport.com.

A shuttle bus connects the airport to the nearby Amtrak station, and limousine (van and bus) service provides door-to-door transportation to and from the airport.

Walking tours of the airport are provided through the marketing office for groups of twelve to thirty people, with a minimum age of nine. Usually these are schoolchildren or civic organizations, VIP groups, or special-interest groups such as firefighters or engineers who receive a "behind the scenes" tour. Individuals who want an airport tour may call to see if a group tour is scheduled that they could join. The normal tour includes visits to and explanations of the baggage claim area, airline ticket counters, restaurants, gift shops, gate departure areas, the National Weather Service, and all the major concourses. Call at least a week to ten days ahead for group tours; the telephone is (301) 261–1000 from the Washington, D.C., area or (410) 859–7026 from elsewhere.

When airport construction was started on May 4, 1947, the airport site was known as Friendship, and many old homes and farms on the 3,200-acre tract were demolished. Only Rezin Howard Hammond's home was left standing, where it remains today at the edge of the airport. Originally known as Cedar Farm because of the cedar trees on the property, it was built in 1820 from bricks made of clay dug on the farm.

It is now the **Benson-Hammond House** and is used by the Anne Arundel County Historical Society, whose purpose is to encourage the appreciation among the general public of "the smaller centers of culture where so much of our heritage lies hidden."

Within the house are a collection of dolls, a display of tokens known as picker checks (made of aluminum, fiberboard, and brass stamped into various shapes and used as currency by farmers, each of whom had his own set of checks with his initials), a miniature replica of Angel's Store in Pasadena, and a growing library of historical and genealogical materials on the second floor. The museum is open for tours on special occasions, and the library is open Thursday from 10:00 A.M. to 3:00 P.M. A user's fee of $1.00 per day is charged for nonmembers.

The Browse and Buy Shoppe is also located at the house; it is open for the same Thursday hours and other times as volunteers are available. Call the Benson-Hammond House (at Aviation Boulevard and Andover Road) at (410) 768–9518 for tours and additional information.

A second Browse and Buy Shoppe is located at **Jones Station,** at the corner of Old Annapolis and Jones Station roads. This late nineteenth-century building was one of the "step-down transformer" power stations for one of the two railroads serving Annapolis. There are no railroads performing that function these days; reportedly, Annapolis is the only state capital without such service. Hours at the Browse and Buy Shoppe are Tuesday through Saturday, 10:00 A.M. to 3:00 P.M.; call (410) 544–3370.

Visitors to Annapolis have a treat in store for them. Annapolis is full of authentic colonial architecture; Colonial Williamsburg in Virginia had to re-create that which is already here. Annapolis is called a "museum without walls" because of the dozens of eighteenth-century buildings in the city, but Annapolitans are quick to point out that it is a living museum, not an artificial one.

Annapolis is Old World charm, the United States Naval Academy, sailboats and powerboats by the hundreds (168,000 boats were registered in Maryland in 1984), antiques shops, taverns, and, most of all, narrow, winding, hilly, and brick-paved streets that invite walking and exploring.

The ◆**Banneker-Douglass Museum** is installed in a handsome Victorian-Gothic structure that was the Mount Moriah

African Methodist Episcopal Church. The church served the community from 1874 until 1971. The museum is named for Benjamin Banneker (mathematician, scientist, astronomer, and surveyor) and Frederick Douglass (writer, journalist, civil libertarian, abolitionist, and U.S. minister and consul general to Haiti), both of whom were born and lived in Maryland. Banneker was appointed to serve on a commission that surveyed and laid out the capital. He had such a phenomenal memory that he produced, in detail, Pierre L'Enfant's plans for the District of Columbia when L'Enfant left—with the plans—before the job was finished.

There are rotating displays within the Hall of National Greatness, the Gallery of Black Maritime History, the Herbert M. Frisby Hall (Frisby was a Baltimore science educator, war correspondent for African-American newspapers, and explorer who made twenty-one trips to the Arctic region and was the second black explorer to reach the North Pole), and the reference library. The museum features African-American arts and crafts, lectures, and films, all to encourage a better understanding of the contributions of African-Americans to Maryland and the United States. Today's legacy is represented by such prominent black artists as Josephine Gross, Gerald Hawkes, Laurence Hurst, and Hughie Lee-Smith, whose works adorn the walls of the gallery.

The Banneker-Douglass Museum is located at 84 Franklin Street, Annapolis. Hours are Tuesday through Friday 10:00 A.M. to 3:00 P.M. and Saturday noon to 4:00 P.M.; call (410) 974–2893.

In July 1989 some fifteen small, brittle bones, carefully wrapped in yellowed paper, were gently placed in a golden urn and laid to rest in a shady cemetery plot near St. Mary's Church in Annapolis. In mid-1987 the Reverend John Murray of St. Mary's had found these **remains of St. Justin,** who was beheaded at the age of twenty-six in the second century A.D.

According to Murray, it is not unusual for churches in Europe to have special tombs containing the relics of saints or martyrs, but few churches in the United States can claim such items because the country is so young. St. Justin's remains arrived in Baltimore in 1873 so the Reverend Joseph Wissel could protect them while Italy was in the middle of a political upheaval. Reverend Wissel and those who followed him displayed them prominently, but during the 1960s the church was renovated and the remains were placed in a box in a church safe.

27

The St. Mary's Church gardens are open to the public periodically during the year; the dates are advertised in the local newspapers. Call Dr. Robert Worden in the evening for additional information (410–263–2396). There are many interesting things to see at the **U.S. Naval Academy.** Start with a visit to the Armel-Leftwich Visitors Center, with a movie and displays about life as a midshipman. You can then explore on your own or take a one-hour-and-ten-minute guided tour. The hours of operation vary according to the day and the season, but the noon tour departs at 11:45 to see the Noon Meal Formation. The center is closed Thanksgiving, Christmas, and New Year's days.

One of the most fascinating exhibits in Annapolis is the display of model ships at the ◈ **U.S. Naval Academy Museum,** which features the work of Henry Huddleston Rogers and Robert F. Sumrall, an extraordinary model builder. Sumrall is the curator charged with repairing and maintaining a fleet of 225 little ships, some of them more than 300 years old. Sumrall built his first model when he was six and went on to be a naval architect, author, historian, model builder, and one of the most highly regarded authorities on ship models and model construction.

Sumrall has built models of significant and famous Maryland ships, including the *Dolphin,* the *Pride of Baltimore,* the *J. T. Leonard* (a unique oyster dredger), and the skipjack *Minnie V.* Most of the work Sumrall does for the academy museum is in the realm of repair, maintenance, and restoration. His creative work, such as the commission for a 6-foot-tall model of the skipjack *Stanley Norman* (the original of which still operates on the Chesapeake) for the Occidental Restaurant in Washington, D.C., he does at home. He also has done an interpretive model of the *Arizona* wreck for the National Park Service memorial at Pearl Harbor, and he is doing another of the Japanese flagship *Akagi.* Private collections, which are located in Coronado, Virginia Beach, New York, and a gallery in Old Town Alexandria, hold his battleship *Wisconsin* and several destroyers.

You'll also want to see Bone Ships, which were crafted by prisoners of war on frigates from meat bones. They are intricate and accurate portrayals of the fighting ships of the times.

The Naval Academy Museum provides a valuable and convenient reference source for studying naval history. The museum is open 9:00 A.M. to 4:50 P.M. Monday through Saturday and 11:00 A.M. to 4:50 P.M. Sunday. Call (410) 267–2108. The skipjack is the symbol of the Chesapeake Bay waterman. These boats were developed in the 1890s, and they are the last surviving commercial sailing fleet in the United States. The oysterdredging boats have become an endangered species, as their number has dwindled from about 1,500 at the turn of the century to about eighty on the water in 1958 and about three dozen in working condition now.

Annapolis has always been a vital area for commerce and trade, particularly when it comes to importing and exporting goods. But it played one of its most unusual commercial roles in 1862, when it became the major depot in the East for holding exchanged prisoners of war. Prisoners were held here until their back pay (earned during their incarceration) could be given to them.

At first they were camped at St. John's College, but the eight small, wooden barracks were inadequate for groups as large as 6,000 men at one time. Two hundred and fifty acres of farmland outside Annapolis were rented from Charles S. and Ann Rebecca Welch for $125 per month. The forty-four barracks and all other buildings were sold at auction some time after 1865, when all the prisoners had been released. All that remains of this mustering place for Union prisoners, called Camp Parole, is the name of the town, **Parole,** on the western side of Annapolis.

Parts of the Parole shopping mall were demolished in 1996, prior to a new mall being constructed. Per regulations, an archaeological dig was conducted. Hopes were high that they would find remnants of the barracks, but alas, they didn't. They did, however, find pottery shards, glass, and hand-fashioned nails that date the dig to the late seventeenth and early eighteenth centuries.

Of special allure are the **historic inns** of Annapolis, each casting its captivating spell for those who want to sense history while enjoying the pleasures of modern accommodations. Even the names—Governor Calvert House, Robert Johnson House, State House Inn, and Maryland Inn—conjure up thoughts of legendary times and days of heroic deeds.

I have particularly fond memories of the Maryland Inn at Church Circle. It was constructed by Thomas Hyde in 1772 and has operated continuously as an inn since the late eighteenth century. The inn sits on a triangular lot called the "drummer's lot," the area where the town drummer, or crier, told of the day's news in the early eighteenth century. For years the King of France Tavern in the Maryland Inn's cellar has been the best home around for live entertainment. Ethel Ennis, Charlie Byrd, Tim Eyermann, and others have filled its brick-walled room with delightful sounds and good times. In years past, the Maryland Inn was where some of the Maryland legislators met each night after the day's session was over to discuss legislative business.

For information about the inns you can write to Historic Inns of Annapolis, 16 Church Circle, Annapolis 21401, or call (410) 263–2641. The toll-free number is (800) 847–8882.

If you want some lodging that is just a little bit different, you might want to try Janice and Bill Costello's **Chesapeake Bay Lighthouse Bed & Breakfast,** just a few miles north of Annapolis.

This could be the saga of the tail wagging the dog. The Costellos had lived in the area for years. Bill was in the Merchant Marine and Janice sold real estate, and both of them loved being near the water. A choice piece of property became available and they snatched it up. The home needed some updating and Bill wanted a two-car garage. He'd grown to love lighthouses during his ten years with the Merchant Marine and decided he wanted his garage to be topped by a lighthouse. In particular he loved the Thomas Point Lighthouse, a noted screw-piled structure of the Chesapeake Bay. For a few dollars he received the blueprints and modified them slightly for larger dormer windows.

He did all the framing and people were brought in to finish it. Some happenstance comments about bed and breakfast places, how ideal the lighthouse would be, and a few modifications later, and voilà! Now the Costellos are licensed to lease out three rooms, each with its own bath. Feel free to enjoy the waterfront property or launch your canoe or kayak. The shallow (2 to 3 feet), sandy-bottom shoreline precludes bringing your boat up to the Costellos' property.

Chesapeake Bay Lighthouse Bed & Breakfast is located at 1423 Sharps Point Road, Annapolis 21401; call (410) 757–0248.

As long as you're in this neighborhood, you may as well take a drive over to Cantler's, noted for Jimmie Cantler, hospitality, crabs all year, and delicious food since the 1970s. The crab cake and soft-shell crab sandwiches are superb. You can also reach Cantler's from the water.

An unofficial declaration of spring's arrival is the annual **Chesapeake Bay Bridge Walk Day,** held on the first Sunday in May. The walk was first held in 1975 after a Towson, Maryland, scout leader noticed that one span was closed for construction and suggested one span could be closed for a daylong walk. An estimated 50,000 pedestrians as well as people in wheelchairs and on crutches cross the eastbound lanes of the bridge, and the only automobiles and trucks permitted belong to official vehicles and media trucks. Jogging, running, skateboarding, biking, and pets (except Seeing Eye dogs) are prohibited; an early-morning race has been established for those who want to speed across the bridge instead of spending about ninety minutes walking and investigating various expansion joints, girder construction, architectural design, and engineering and assembly facets.

Pedestrians normally are not allowed on the 4½-mile structure connecting the Annapolis area to the large spit of land known as the Eastern Shore. Blue waters lap innocuously about 185 feet below the twin spans of the bridge, also known as the William Preston Lane, Jr., Memorial Bridge.

Parking lots in Annapolis and at Anne Arundel Community College and also on the Eastern Shore start filling up at 8:00 A.M. Buses start taking walkers to the east side at 9:00 A.M. There is no charge for parking, but there is a modest charge for the bus.

One of the newest museums in Maryland is the **Captain Salem Avery House,** which opened its doors in mid-September 1989. Avery's home, in Shady Side, was built in 1860 on the banks of the West River and was purchased by the Shady Side Rural Heritage Society to establish a museum to "protect, document, and illustrate the history and traditions" of Shady Side. The society is particularly pleased that they were able to obtain some of the original Avery furniture from the owners of the house. The Captain Salem Avery House is located at 1418 East West Shady Side Road, Shady Side 20764. The house is open Sunday from 1:00 to 4:00 P.M. You can also call Mavis Daly at (301) 261–5234 to make an appointment.

For additional information about Anne Arundel County, write to Annapolis and Anne Arundel County Conference and Visitors Bureau, 26 West Street, Annapolis 21401. Call (410) 280–0445.

BALTIMORE CITY

Baltimore attractions that deserve space from me and attention from you include the **Great Blacks in Wax Museum** (the only one in the country), 1601 East North Avenue, (410) 563–3404; the Indian Cultural Centre (where you can taste authentic food from India), 110 West Mulberry Street, (410) 528–0333; Baltimore's Holocaust Memorial, located at the corner of Gay and Lombard streets; the Jewish Heritage Center on Lloyd Street, between Lombard and Baltimore streets, (410) 732–6400; and the Baltimore City Conservatory, Druid Lake Drive, (410) 396–1080.

Coverage of the city will include two special city views, a new memorial, the traditional painted screens of East Baltimore, two restaurants, and a number of factory tours.

A spectacular way to start your Baltimore visit is at the ✦ **Top of the World observation deck and museum.** On a clear day you will see an eye-opening, five-sided panoramic view of the city, its harbor, and beyond from the twenty-seventh floor of the tallest pentagonal building in the country, designed by I. M. Pei. Exhibits, films, and audiovisual material will familiarize you with Baltimore's past, present, and future. The World Trade Center is at 401 East Pratt Street. Hours are Monday through Friday 10:00 A.M. to 5:30 P.M., Saturday 10:00 A.M. to 7:00 P.M., and Sunday 11:00 A.M. to 7:00 P.M.; call about extended summer hours. Admission for adults is $2.50; for children 5 to 15 and seniors, $1.50. The phone number is (410) 837–4515.

If you would like an organized or specially designed personal tour, call Ruth Fader at **Baltimore Rent-A-Tour.** Ruth started her business in the early 1970s when she realized no one was giving tours of Baltimore. Now her company conducts about 900 tours a year. Baltimore Rent-A-Tour specializes in the distinctive. My favorite is her insomniac tour, which may take you late at night to see a bakery, nocturnal zoo animals, a television station preparing for the late-news broadcast, and a newspaper preparing the first edition of tomorrow's breakfast companion.

Another is her Halloween tour (costume dressing optional, with best-costume prizes, of course), which may include Edgar Allan Poe's grave and the catacombs at Westminster Church, the ghost of the Shot Tower, and the Baltimore Streetcar Museum, where

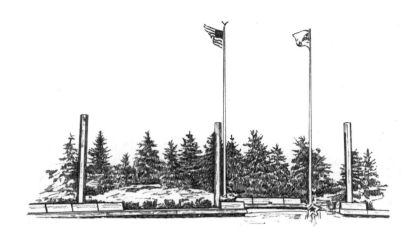

Maryland Vietnam Veterans Memorial

you can ride turn-of-the-century trolleys. This tour ends with a fine view of the sunrise from the "Top of the World" at the Trade Center. Surely you have the idea by now. Contact Baltimore Rent-A-Tour at 3414 Philip Drive, Baltimore 21208, or call (410) 653–2998.

On May 28, 1989, the ◆ **Maryland Vietnam Veterans Memorial** was dedicated to the memory of 1,046 Marylanders who were killed or became missing in action in the Vietnam conflict. The names and inscriptions are readable whether one is standing, in a wheelchair, or at a child's-eye level. The veterans' names are etched into granite, along with this inscription:

> MARYLANDERS, WHILE IN THIS PLACE, PAUSE TO RECALL OUR NATION'S IDEALS, ITS PROMISE, ITS ABUNDANCE, AND OUR CONTINUING RESPONSIBILITIES TOWARD THE SHARED FULFILL- MENT OF OUR ASPIRATIONS. REMEMBER, TOO, THOSE WHOSE EXERTIONS AND SACRIFICES UNDERLIE THESE BLESSINGS. REMEMBER, INDEED, THE LIVING AND THE DEAD.

Funds were raised by Maryland veterans who called themselves "The Last Patrol." They marched across the state during sweltering August heat in 1986, from Oakland in western Maryland to Ocean City in the east, and another 200 miles from Point Lookout to Baltimore the next year. Architect Paul Spreiregan designed the monument. It stands beside the Patapsco River in Middle Branch Park, off Route 2.

Old Baltimore has long been known for its blocks and blocks of row houses, with their brightly scrubbed white marble steps. Almost as historic, but not nearly as well known, are the ❖ **painted screens** for windows and doors that decorate the houses lining the streets of East Baltimore.

It is said that William Oktavec painted the first screen on a hot summer day in 1913. His fresh produce was wilting in the heat, so he took it inside and painted groceries on the screens to show his customers what he had available. When you understand that this area is all cement and brick, with very little greenery, no front yards, and few gardens or trees, you can appreciate the thoughts some had about providing a little colorful decoration. Another advantage of the painted screens is that windows and doors can be left open for the breezes because the paint allows those who are inside to look out, but outsiders cannot see in.

People started painting on the screens pictures of red-roofed bungalows and ponds with ducks or swans swimming around in them. There are rainbows and religious scenes, but mostly the artwork reflects the memories of the inhabitants' home countries in Europe and scenes of a new life in America. The scenes depicted the single-family, country-cottage homes of the sort everyone dreamed of owning.

For the best screen viewing, start at Haussner's Restaurant (see below) and travel along both sides of Eastern Avenue. The Hatton Senior Center, at the corner of Fait and South Linwood Avenue, has screens in each of its twenty windows. Remember, this generally is a seasonal display, with the screens in place between May and October.

Six or seven screen painters remain, but they are in their fifties or older. They still work away at it, saying "Practice makes perfect and perfect practice makes art."

You can have a screen painted for about $20 and up, even if you do not live in or visit Baltimore. Write the Painted Screen Society of Baltimore, Box 12122, Baltimore 21281.

Although there are many restaurants of note in Baltimore

neighborhoods, including Fell's Point, Little Italy, Charles Street's Restaurant Row, and, of course, Harborplace, I will highlight just two of my favorites. Both are classics. Taking them alphabetically (the only fair way), I'll start with **Attman's Delicatessen.** This deli, established in 1915, is the place to go for corned beef sandwiches, knishes, beef barley and mushroom soup ("Bubbie's best"), Dr. Brown's celery tonic, and Attman's "World-Famous Jumbo Kosher Hot Dogs served the way you like it . . . on real Jewish seeded roll." This is not a kosher delicatessen—you can also find crab soup and Reuben sandwiches among the menu selections and the shop is open on Saturday—but it has the feel of one. The store is narrow, crowded, busy, and smells seductively delicious. The choices are puzzling; what do you order first, and should you eat in or carry out?

Attman's Delicatessen, 1019 East Lombard Street, Baltimore 21202, is open 8:00 A.M. to 7:00 P.M. daily; call (410) 563–2666. No credit cards are accepted. Attman's can also be found at Owings Mills Town Center, 2106 Mill Run Circle, Owings Mills 21117 (410–363–1661) and Pomona Square, Pikesville 21208 (410–484–8477).

My other favorite is **Haussner's,** where the menu has more than one hundred entrées, many of them German specialties. Inspirational desserts are available here or to take home, if you could begin to eat dessert after one of their meals. But Haussner's is equally famous for its extensive original art and antiques display.

People have been coming to this family-owned and -operated restaurant since 1926 to dine and view the paintings, etchings, china, and sculpture by some of Europe's renowned masters. Here you can enjoy Baltimore's largest privately owned art collection and feast on German-American and seafood delicacies. Imagine dining with Rembrandt, Gainsborough, and Whistler! At Haussner's, you can.

Haussner's is located at 3242 Eastern Avenue, Baltimore 21224; call (410) 327–8365. Reservations are accepted for lunch only. Hours are Tuesday through Saturday from 11:00 A.M. to 11:00 P.M.

Now, on to a few fascinating factory tours.

The ◆ **General Motors Baltimore Assembly Plant** turns out GMC Safaris and Chevrolet Astros at the rate of nearly one a minute, twenty hours a day, five days a week. In a cavernous room split by railroad tracks and boxcars, you can watch a flat piece of stamped sheet metal, instrument panel shells, heater controls, windshields, roofs, carpet (watching water nozzles cut carpet is really interesting), engines, and all the other components come together to form a car.

It is a throbbing, pulsating, noisy, smelly operation, but big and little engineers love to watch it. The tour follows a one-and-a-half-mile-long assembly line and takes about ninety minutes; tours are offered weekdays at 9:00 A.M. and 7:30 P.M. They accept a maximum of fifty people and advise that no cameras are allowed and no open-toe shoes or sandals should be worn. Children must be ten or older, and safety glasses are provided. Reservations with three weeks' notice are requested and can be made by calling Bill McGonigle at (410) 631–2508 or by writing General Motors Baltimore Assembly Plant, P.O. Box 148, 2122 Broening Highway, Baltimore 21203. The plant is located near Sparrows Point. Take I–95 north to Fort McHenry Tunnel, turn right at Boston Street (the first exit after the tunnel), and right again on Broening Highway.

The **Eagle Coffee Company,** one of the few independent coffee-roasting companies in the United States, sells about one million pounds of coffee a year. You can watch (and smell) the coffee roasting and packaging processes. The free, hour-long tours are offered weekdays by appointment, with twenty-five people maximum. Call Jacqueline Parris at Eagle Coffee Company, 1019-27 Hillen Street, Baltimore at (410) 685–5893.

The ✦**Calvert Distilling Company** lets you follow the preparation of fine whiskey, vodka, and gin from distillation through the bottling process to quality control. The tour includes a view of the warehouses filled with the finished product and a sampling from a lab technician. Call (410) 247–1000 to reserve a free ninety-minute tour. A maximum of fifty people are permitted on the tour, which is given weekdays by appointment only at the House of Seagram, 5001 Washington Boulevard, Baltimore 21227.

The last tour is through the offices of the Pulitzer prize–winning daily newspaper the *Baltimore Sun.* Follow the frantic process from newsroom to composing room to press room. One-hour tours are offered Monday, Wednesday, and Thursday at 9:30 A.M., 11:00 A.M., and 1:00 P.M. by appointment. There is no charge, but your request must be in writing, and they accept no more than thirty people per tour. They do not accept children below the fourth-grade level. Stuart Boytilla is the person to contact; the best time to call him is between 3:00 and 4:00 P.M. The *Baltimore Sun* offices are at 501 North Calvert Street, Baltimore 21278 (410–332–6222).

Kirk Stieff and Moore's Candies no longer offer tours because of insurance restrictions. If you see brochures advertising the tours, disregard them.

Public transportation around Baltimore City has become pretty convenient in the last few years. The trolley system is good and inexpensive. The subway system is also fine.

There's also **Ed Kane's Water Taxi** that goes to almost every popular waterfront attraction, including Harborplace, the Maryland Science Center, the National Aquarium in Baltimore, the Baltimore Museum of Industry, Fell's Point, and Little Italy. Thus, you can park for the day and take the water taxi around to various spots you want to visit, not having to worry about finding parking places, having correct change, or fighting traffic. Adult fare is $3.50; the fare for children 10 and under accompanied by an adult is $2.25. These prices cover unlimited use on the day of purchase. Call (800) 658–8947 for the daily operating schedule.

Another option is the **light-rail system,** taking you from the suburbs to Oriole Park at Camden Yards and back again for less expense and aggravation than driving into the city and parking. It runs from Glen Burnie to Timonium, with stops in downtown Baltimore, including Camden Yards. It operates every fifteen minutes from 6:00 A.M. to 11:00 P.M. Monday through Friday, every fifteen minutes from 8:00 A.M. to 11:00 P.M. on Saturday, and every thirty minutes from 11:00 A.M. to 7:00 P.M. on Sunday. Hours are extended or modified during the baseball season. Free parking is available at designated light-rail stops, and all light-rail trains are handicapped accessible.

By spring 1997, extensions should be complete to Baltimore-Washington International Airport, Penn Station, and Hunt Valley Mall. The cost is $1.35 per trip, $2.70 for a round-trip, or $3.00 for an all-day pass that's good on the subway, the bus system, and the light-rail. Call (410) 539–5000.

For additional Baltimore information, write the Baltimore Area

Visitors Center, Pier One, Constellation Dock, Baltimore 21202, or call (800) 282–6632 or (410) 837–4636.

BALTIMORE COUNTY

Two post office mural selections are of interest here. The first is in **Catonsville,** where in 1942 Avery Johnson painted five scenes of historic note, entitled "Incidents of History of Catonsville." The murals start with Indians, go on to farmers rolling tobacco in hogsheads to market, and then depict the romance of Richard Caton and Mary "Holly" Carroll. Holly, the daughter of Declaration of Independence signer Charles Carroll, was only sixteen when Caton proposed. Her father refused because he said Caton had a reputation for not paying his debts. Caton prevailed, and they were married in 1788. Charles Carroll built a house for them, Castle Thunder, on Frederick Road, where the library is now; then he built a newer home in Green Spring Valley (that home still stands). The last panel shows Caton, Holly, and Charles Carroll with his plans for the town of Catonsville.

Several years ago the post office roof began to leak, and that did not bode well for the plaster walls or the paintings. The late Thomas Cockey, whose family also goes back to the eighteenth century, decided the murals should be repaired. Federal officials balked at the $35,000 repair bill, but Cockey (as in the town of Cockeysville, also in Baltimore County) and the Historical Society prevailed. A plaque documenting the story depicted in the panels has been installed by the society.

The **Towson Post Office murals** caused a real ruckus. Nicolai Cikovsky, a Russian-born, naturalized citizen, was an artist who lived in Washington, D.C. In 1939 he gave the postmaster, at the postal official's request, a series of panels depicting "Milestones in American Transportation." The populace took one look and cried foul. They declared the subject of the paintings was trite, derivative, and clichéd. They also were upset by inaccuracies, such as a wagon pulled by horses without reins, smokestack smoke going the wrong direction, a train looking like a model railroad engine rather than a real locomotive, and a gun holster worn backward.

This was the work of a painter who had studied at several distinguished schools in Russia, taught in the United States at the

Corcoran Gallery, and sold paintings to the Chicago Art Institute, the Whitney Museum of American Art, and numerous other celebrated galleries across the country. The residents thought the paintings looked like bad "B" movie posters, at best. They wanted murals that reflected the life and history of Towson, and they wanted the artist to visit the area; often artists went to see the location where their paintings would hang. Of course, many murals that depicted localities were not necessarily accurate; one in Barre, Vermont, shows men working in the quarries on stone that has never been found in Vermont and with tools that were never used in Vermont. The Prince George's County mural in Upper Marlboro, Maryland, is another example. The upshot is that the errors were corrected, and the murals stayed. They can still be found at 101 West Chesapeake Avenue, Towson—no longer the main post office but the finance office.

◆ **Wild Acres Trail,** a mile-long wildlife habitat demonstration trail in Owings Mills, was opened in late 1989 in the seventy-two–acre Gwynnbrook Wildlife Management Area. It features twenty-three ways to help gardeners and wildlife watchers invite birds, butterflies, and other animals to their property. Trail maps are available for the self-guided tour, and the trail is open from dawn to dusk daily except on Wednesday. No pets are allowed.

Included along the trail are a backyard pond and rock garden; a bee, butterfly, and hummingbird garden; nesting structures for birds and squirrels; bird feeders; and a variety of garden plants that produce fruit eaten by all sorts of animals. Other examples are shown for owners of large properties.

More than 120 kinds of birds live in or visit the Gwynnbrook area, making bird-watching a marvelous recreational attraction. Photo opportunities are wondrous because of the wildflowers that bloom in the spring and fall.

At Towson State University, in the Fine Arts Center, is the ◆ **Asian Arts Center** at the Roberts Gallery, named in honor of Frank Roberts, who donated a large number of Asian artifacts and artworks to start this collection. Changing and permanent displays of Asian, African, and pre-Columbian works are featured. Concerts, films, lectures, and workshops are sponsored throughout the school year.

The Asian Arts Center is open June through August, Monday through Friday 11:00 A.M. to 3:00 P.M. and September through

May, Monday through Friday 10:00 A.M. to 4:00 P.M. No admission is charged. Groups are welcome by appointment. Call (410) 830–2807.

The ❖ **Oregon Ridge Park and Nature Center** is a great place to take a break after hours of driving and seeing regular tourist attractions. Within its 836 acres are a number of marked trails of varying length and difficulty, downhill and cross-country skiing areas, a greenhouse, an archaeological research site, an outdoor stage, and a launching site for hang gliders.

Starting in the nature center, you can see how a honeybee hive works, look at local flowers and plants in the greenhouse, or check on such live animals as fish, frogs, mice, salamanders, snakes, and Stubby, the pet opposum, all native to the park. A huge tree exhibit reveals the various parts of the forest ecosystem, from the worms and moles living among the roots and underbrush to the owls and hawks perching in its highest limbs. The area's history is depicted by artifacts retrieved from archaeological digs in the park. These items were reclaimed from the digs by students in the Baltimore County public school system. Students also constructed a full-scale replica of an 1850s storage shed, set on its original foundation outside the nature center.

The nature trails crisscross the park, so a hiker sees the natural interactions of birds, fields, ponds, streams, swamps, wildlife, and woods. For those who like nature on the cultured side, summer concerts are presented here by the Baltimore Symphony.

Oregon Ridge Park and Nature Center, Beaver Dam Road, is reached by the Shawan Road Exit 20-B off I–83; go west 1 mile, turn left on Beaver Dam Road, bear right at the fork, and follow the signs. Call (410) 771–0034 for more information.

❖ **Ashland Furnace** is one of the six relatively easily reached furnaces in Maryland (the others are Catoctin Furnace, Lonaconing Iron Furnace, Antietam, Principio in Cecil County, and Nassawango in Worcester County). Said to have been named for the Kentucky home of Henry Clay, Ashland's three furnaces, engine room, and casting house were kept functioning from around 1844 to 1893. Originally there were also large storage buildings for raw materials and a village with a school, church, store, and about five dozen houses.

The ore was mined in Phoenix, Glencoe, Riderwood, Texas, Oregon Ridge, and other parts of what is now north-central Baltimore County. Now the area is mined by a developer, and the Strutt Group has incorporated about a dozen of the old village's buildings. The office and mid-nineteenth century store, the school, several houses, and a group of dwellings called Stone Row have been renovated and assimilated into the industrial site. The old Ashland Presbyterian Church, near the gates of the new community, is still an active place of worship.

Ashland Furnace is east on Paper Mill Road from York Road, just north of Cockeysville.

For additional tourism information write to Office of Promotion and Tourism, 23 West Chesapeake Avenue, Towson 21204, or call (410) 887–8040.

CARROLL COUNTY

This county was named for Charles Carroll, an American Revolutionary War leader and Maryland signer of the Declaration of Independence.

If you find yourself in Carroll County, most likely you are driving along I–70 to or from Baltimore, or you are here to visit the **Carroll County Farm Museum.**

This complex has a general store that's reminiscent of the 1800s and sells items handcrafted by Farm Museum artisans, souvenirs, nickel candies, and much more. Among the activities scheduled on the grounds are a Civil War Encampment (19th Georgia Regiment), a day honoring Older Americans Month, a fiddlers' convention, a day devoted to antique farm machinery, and a day to celebrate Maryland wines. General admission is $3.00 for adults, $2.00 for those twelve to eighteen and sixty and over, and free for those under twelve. Group tours and rates are available. The museum is open weekends May through October from noon to 5:00 P.M. and Tuesday through Friday in July and August from 10:00 A.M. to 4:00 P.M. Call (800) 654–4645.

Carroll County's streams, valleys, farms, woodlands, and villages provide an ideal backdrop for exploring off the highway, and an ideal way to do that is by bicycle. ❿ **Bicycle tours** have been designed by resident cyclists outlining ten of their favorite routes, ranging from short to long and easy to challenging. Each route is on a separate map with its own description of the tour. Brochures are available at the visitor center in Westminster.

41

For examples, the Taneytown route is nearly 14 miles long with a moderately hilly ride. It starts at Taneytown Memorial Park, "where a public pool and picnic grounds offer warm-weather possibilities. Your tour heads toward Littlestown, Pennsylvania, and winds through rustic areas where deer and pheasants abound. Pick out an early Christmas tree at one of the tree farms, or stop and listen to the ripplings of Pipe Creek. Wind back through the alleys of Taneytown and by the beautiful Fish and Game Club pond."

The New Windsor tour has rolling hills and is 8 miles long. "Wind through the beautiful Wakefield Valley on your way past Robert Strawbridge's Home (birthplace of American Methodism). This ride offers splendid country scenery, picturesque eighteenth- and nineteenth-century homes, and an opportunity to stop at the New Windsor Service Center and visit its unique International Gift Shop."

According to local legend, you and I are not the only visitors to Carroll County. Several apparitions also frequent the countryside, and you may even meet a friendly one. The first of the ❖ **Ghosts of Carroll County** is at the Shellman House, 210 East Main Street, Westminster. A little girl in white, they say, delights at having visitors stop by the visitor center, located at the Historical Society of Carroll County. Spirits, in addition to the liquid kind, are said to reside at Cockey's Tavern, 216 East Main Street; since the early 1800s this tavern has been the site of political rallies for Andrew Jackson, antitax meetings, fancy balls, and all-night debauchery.

At Main and Court streets, the ghosts of slaves supposedly return to the Carroll County auction block where slave trading was done in pre-Revolutionary War times. Other specters have been reported at Ascension churchyard, the courthouse, the old Westminster jail, Western Maryland College (Levine Hall has a musical ghost), and Avondale—the home of Legh Master, the most celebrated of Carroll's ghosts—on Stone Chapel Road in Wakefield Valley. It is said that Master was a tyrant, a miser, a lecher, and a cad. Two Confederate ghosts reportedly visit the last remaining building of Irving College on Grafton Street, and during a full moon, an Indian walks along a ridge in the tiny town of Lineboro.

For those of you who choose to pursue these nocturnal visitors, talk with the Historical Society in general (through the Office of Promotion and Tourism) and Amos Davidson, a local historian, in particular. Additional tourism information is available from the Carroll County Office of Tourism. Write to them at 125 North Court Street, Westminster 21157, or call (800) 876–2085.

CECIL COUNTY

If you have seen such movies as *The Manchurian Candidate, Guys & Dolls, The Philadelphia Story, Pillow Talk,* and *Solid Gold Cadillac,* then you have heard people talking about eloping to **Elkton** or going to "that town in Maryland" to get married. Until the late thirties, the town of Elkton was known as the marriage capital of the world. Some 10,000 people a year were wed here, and one assumes most of them were eloping. They came to Elkton because it was the first county seat south of New York and other northeastern areas that did not require a waiting period or blood test before the ceremony was performed.

Only one wedding chapel remains, the ✤**Little Wedding Chapel.** This is where Babe Ruth and Joan Fontaine were married, among dozens of notables, and this is where nearly 1,000 couples are still married each year. Stop by to talk with Barbara Foster and hear some of her many stories, witness a wedding or two, or plan for your own nuptials to be held here.

The Little Wedding Chapel is located at 142 East Main Street, Elkton 21921. The phone number is (410) 398–3640.

As long as we are on a romantic subject, we can visit two ✤**covered bridges** (or "kissing" bridges) in Cecil. There was a time when Cecil and Frederick counties vied for the most covered bridges in the state, but few remain.

Gilpin's Falls covered bridge has a 119-foot span and a 13½-foot roadway, and it is adjacent to Route 272 over Northeast Creek, a half-mile north of Bayview. Reportedly, the bridge's arches were made from single timbers, which were curved to shape by balancing them on stumps and pulling their ends down. The bridge was constructed in the 1850s, abandoned in the 1930s, and left to disintegrate until 1959, when it was restored. Traffic along Route 272 bypasses the bridge, which is within a few yards of the roadway.

Gilpin's Falls covered bridge is on Route 272, 5 miles north of the town of North East, or 2 miles north of I–95.

The second covered bridge is at Fair Hill, which was a 7,000-acre estate owned by William DuPont, Jr. The entire Maryland portion, more than 5,000 acres, was purchased by the state as a Natural Resource Area. In the northern reaches of the property, near the Pennsylvania border, is the 1850s covered bridge, which has been on private property for years. Until recently, to find it you had to wander through Fair Hill Condominiums (for thoroughbred racehorses) along roads posted against trespassers and hope you could find your way through the twists and turns and lack of directional signs.

Ed Walls manages Fair Hills Natural and Environmental Center, a facility located in the northern half of the 5,600-acre **Fair Hill Natural Resources Management Area** in northeastern Cecil County. The headquarters building was formerly used by William DuPont, Jr., as his hunting lodge and is next to a covered bridge over Big Elk Creek. There are two Mason–Dixon line markers on the property.

This is an outdoor education school with programs designed to encourage awareness, understanding, and appreciation of the natural world, our natural resources, and the impact of people on the environment. The indoor and outdoor classrooms are open Monday through Friday from 8:30 A.M. to 5:00 P.M. and on occasional weekends and evenings for members of the Fair Hill Environmental Foundation, Inc. (a private, nonprofit support group) and for groups by reservation. Program subjects might include bird identification, wildflowers, marsh studies, and landscaping.

Across Route 273 is the steeplechase track at Fair Hill, an exact replica of Aintree, where England's Grand National is held. Since it opened in 1933, there have been a number of steeplechase races annually, and the May and October events are the only steeplechase races in the United States that permit pari-mutuel wagering. Fair Hill is also the home of the National Steeplechase and Hunt Association, which moved from Belmont, New York, in June 1989.

Fair Hill Natural Resource Management Area is at the junction of Route 273 and Route 213, Fair Hill 21921. Call (410) 398–1246.

The Mitchell House is a two-and-a-half–story stone dwelling believed to have been built in 1764 (based on a fireback date), though it has had considerable alterations since then; it is the location of the ◆ **Fair Hill Inn.** The house has been a Revolutionary War hospital (run by its owner, Dr. Abraham Mitchell) for Continental soldiers, a hotel, a post office, and a store. Mr. and Mrs. Anthony Graziano purchased it from the State of Maryland in 1978 when it was in dilapidated condition, and they have proudly restored it.

Now the house is a fine restaurant that features an Italian continental menu but specializes in Maryland seafood. Just perusing the menu, which includes Veal Imperial (a Fair Hill delight), Pasta Marinara (scallops, shrimp, clams, and mussels served over pasta), and Seafood Beatrice (lobster tail, scallops, shrimp, and crabmeat cooked with brandy, flamed with Pernod, for two), is enough to encourage *buon appetito*.

The Fair Hill Inn is open for lunch Tuesday through Friday from 11:30 A.M. to 2:30 P.M., for dinner Tuesday through Sunday from 5:00 to 9:00 P.M., and for Sunday brunch from 11:30 A.M. to 2:30 P.M. Reservations are advised; call (410) 398–4187. The inn is located at the junction of Routes 273 and 213, Fair Hill 21921.

At one time there were two covered bridges crossing the Susquehanna River, but the last one was flooded with the construction of the ❖**Conowingo Hydroelectric Plant.** Built in 1928, Conowingo is one of the largest hydroelectric plants in the northeast, if not in the country. The enormous dam forms a freshwater lake 14 miles long, impounding some 105 billion gallons of water. It is a noted freshwater fishing spot.

The best part is that you can see the plant tick. On weekends you don't need an appointment; just show up at the entrance below the station on the downriver side at 9:30 A.M., 11:00 A.M., 1:00 P.M., or 2:30 P.M. Somebody will be there to show you through the dam, where you will see the generators, pumps, air tanks, water pipelines, transformers, circuit breakers, high-tension wires, and all kinds of electrical equipment. Children must be twelve or older to take the entire tour, but younger children will be allowed to see part of the operation. You should not wear high heels because there are a lot of grates to walk over.

Daily and group tour reservations should be made a week or more in advance, and groups should be no larger than forty people. The tour must be taken between 8:00 A.M. and 4:00 P.M., so you should schedule the one-hour-plus tour no later than 2:30 P.M. Call the recreation office at (410) 457–5011. The address is Conowingo Dam, P.O. Box 237, Conowingo 21918.

Established in 1876, the ❖**Day Basket Factory** in the town of North East still makes oak splint baskets the old-fashioned way. Shortly after the Civil War, Edward and Samuel Day came to

North East from Massachusetts to make their baskets because the wood was plentiful, the transportation was good, and the demand for their wares, particularly from cotton pickers, was great.

Business boomed, and during World War I the factory had thirty-five people on its payroll turning out 2,000 baskets a week. In November 1989 Robert and Virginia McKnight, Dean Richwine, Theodore Lambert III, and Gary Sorrelle bought the factory. There are four or five basket makers there who produce old-time baskets, from lunch and market styles to fruit and bread baskets. Hobbyists will be pleased to know they have pliable number 1 oak strips, hand-split in any dimension, for chair seats or baskets or whatever you need.

You can watch the process (you must be at least eighteen) Monday through Friday 8:30 A.M. to 4:00 P.M. The store is open on Saturday, but on that day there are no workers there. Please call ahead (410–287–6100) to let them know if you want a tour. The factory, located at the corner of Irishtown Road and Mauldin Avenue, North East 21901, is closed in January and February.

Plumpton Park Zoo, the second-largest zoo in Maryland, is a rural zoological garden that features plants as well as exotic and native animals, including emu, wallabies, llamas, bison, Persian sheep, Chinese deer, miniature donkeys, pygmy goats, wild turkeys, and Australian black swans in a country setting. Eighteenth-century buildings and ruins are on the grounds, including the 1734 mill that houses the gift shop. The zoo has an adopt-an-animal program, with prices ranging from $10 for an African goose to $100 for a zebra.

Plumpton Park Zoo is open from 10:00 A.M. to 5:00 P.M. daily. Admission for adults is $4.00, for seniors $2.00, and for children $2.75. Group tours are available. Contact the zoo at 1416 Telegraph Road (Route 273), Rising Sun 21911, or call (410) 658–6850.

With more than 200 miles of tidal shoreline, dozens of marinas, and acres of waterfront parks, all poised at the top of Chesapeake Bay, it is easy to understand the importance of the estuary in the history of this county. The creation of the **Chesapeake and Delaware Canal** on October 17, 1829, made water transportation in this area even more important. At that time the canal had four locks, but the Corps of Army Engineers lowered the canal to sea level in 1927.

Receiving considerably less publicity than the C & O Canal, the 13-mile C & D Canal cuts off some 350 miles of water navigation for ships going between Philadelphia and Baltimore, and the 22,000 vessels that use it annually make it one of the busiest waterways in the world. A museum in Chesapeake City, located next to the canal, reviews its history. The museum is open Monday through Saturday from 8:00 A.M. to 4:15 P.M. and Sunday from 10:00 A.M. to 6:00 P.M. It is closed on Sunday from Thanksgiving through Easter. Call (410) 885–5622 for more information.

I find the other, or north, side of the canal equally interesting. During the ride or walk across the bridge, 135 feet in the air, you can see the canal's course for miles in both directions. From the north side you can see the pilots on their pilot boats going to and from the ships navigating the canal. Stop by the Pilot House for information and a schedule on ships coming through.

For additional information, write to Karen Emery, Tourism Coordinator, Cecil County Chamber of Commerce, 1 East Main Street, Elkton 21921, or call (800) CECIL–95.

HARFORD COUNTY

Harford County goes from covered bridge to lighthouse, which explains the variety of features you will find here. One of the remaining covered bridges in Maryland connects Harford and Baltimore counties and crosses over Gunpowder Falls. The ❖ **Jericho Covered Bridge** was constructed between 1850 and 1860 and measures 88 feet, with a 14⅔-foot roadway. Steel beams, steel stringers, steel crosstie rods, and bottom chord were installed later for reinforcement, and today it remains in good condition. To reach the bridge, take Route 152 from exit 74 of I–95, turn left onto Jerusalem Road and proceed to Jericho Road.

Havre de Grace (pronounced as it is spelled, not with a French pronunciation) is the home of one of the oldest continuously used lighthouses on the East Coast. The **Concord Point Light** was constructed in 1827 but decommissioned in 1975; it was later vandalized but is now in tip-top shape. You can climb the twenty-eight steps plus six steps on a ladder and see an impressive view of the Susquehanna River and Chesapeake Bay.

The lighthouse is open on Saturday and Sunday afternoons from 1:00 to 5:00 P.M. May through October, or by appointment. It is located at the foot of Lafayette Street in Havre de Grace. The phone numbers are (410) 939–1340 and 939–2016. From the lighthouse you can walk the half-mile to Tydings Park via a new promenade (boardwalk) along the shore of the Chesapeake Bay.

Another interesting attraction is the Susquehanna Museum of Havre de Grace, which tells you about the southern terminus of the Susquehanna and Tidewater Canal. The museum's address is P.O. Box 253, Havre de Grace 21078; the phone number is (410) 939–5780.

A self-guided tour brochure is available from Harford County Tourism in Bel Air; it highlights a sample of the 800 structures that contribute to the Havre de Grace Historic District. The buildings range in period from the 1780s through the Canal era (1830–1850) and the Victorian era (1880–1910) to the contemporary.

Havre de Grace is the self-proclaimed decoy capital of the world, and the **Havre de Grace Decoy Museum** has complete collections of decoys by Madison Mitchell and Paul Gibson. An annual Decoy Festival is held about the first weekend of May at the museum and the Havre de Grace Middle and High schools. The Decoy Museum is open daily from 11:00 A.M. to 4:00 P.M. The address is R. Madison Mitchell Place, Post Office Box A, Havre de Grace 21078. Call (410) 939–3739.

About 10 blocks up the road, at Franklin Street and North Union Avenue, is the ◆**Susquehanna Trading Company.** Owner Duane Henry has more than 2,500 old and new Chesapeake Bay decoys on display and locally handcrafted decoys for sale, starting at $9.95. He also features a large selection of waterfowl decorations, including miniature decoys; wildlife-decorated personal, household, and office accessories; limited-edition prints; and decoy lamps. The Susquehanna Trading Company is open seven days a week from 10:00 A.M. to 5:00 P.M. at 322 North Union Avenue, (410) 939–4252.

Crossing the Susquehanna River via Route 40 is the Thomas J. Hatem Memorial Bridge, between Harford and Cecil counties. It opened in 1940 as the Susquehanna River Bridge and was renamed in 1986 to honor Hatem, a prominent Harford County

Concord Point Light

resident who devoted his life to public and civic service. The bridge is 1½ miles long and rises 89 feet above the river, connecting the communities of Havre de Grace and Perryville. More than seven million vehicles use the bridge each year. The toll is $2.00 (northbound only) for passenger cars.

❖ **Liriodendron** is a Palladian-style mansion with Greek columns, French doors, marble walls in the kitchen and bathroom, and thirteen fireplaces; it is now on the National Register of Historic Places. It was built as a palatial summer home in 1898 for Dr. Howard A. Kelly, one of the "Big Four" founders of Baltimore's Johns Hopkins Hospital and Medical School. This historic house museum features changing exhibits and art displays as well as a permanent exhibit of memorabilia from the Kelly Collection. Now it is a cultural center for Harford County, with superb facilities for exhibitions, lectures, and concerts.

Tours are available on Sunday from 1:00 to 5:00 P.M. except on national holidays. Call (410) 838–3942 or 879–4424. The address is Liriodendron, 502 West Gordon Street, Bel Air 21014.

For additional tourism information on Harford County write to Discover Harford County Tourism Council, Inc., Post Office Box 635, Bel Air 21014.

HOWARD COUNTY

Howard County offers tremendous contrasts in lifestyles: from Ellicott City, a former mill town, with its original stone buildings, antiques and specialty shops, historic sites, and B & O (Baltimore and Ohio) Railroad Station Museum; to Columbia, the planned village, with its Merriweather Post Pavilion, huge mall, and Columbia Information Center. As usual, I will cover some of the less-visited and more countrified places.

Although not a covered bridge, the **Bollman Truss Bridge** (1869) is of interest because the red cast-iron, open railroad bridge is the only one of its type in the world. It is said to be the first bridge constructed of iron, as opposed to wood or stone. Restoration of the bridge took place in 1974, near Savage Mill (which is now filled with antiques shops and artists' studios), and there is a nice little park and hiking trails around the bridge. You can find the bridge off Route 1, at Savage, near Savage Mill.

Another bridge of note was and is for trains rather than cars.

The ◆**Thomas Viaduct** (1833) stretches from Baltimore County to Howard County across the Patapsco River. Eight elliptical arches support a 60-foot-high granite block structure, which allowed tall ships to pass under. Just as the Ellicott City Railroad Station has endured as a landmark to the growth of railroading in Maryland, so does the viaduct.

When B & O Railroad officials began looking to expand the railroad south to Washington, D.C., they faced a monumental problem: how to cross the Patapsco River. They solved it with a monumental structure, Thomas Viaduct. Named for Philip Thomas, the first president of the B & O Railroad, it was designed by Baltimorean Benjamin Latrobe, and it was the first curved, stone-arched bridge in America. Construction began July 4, 1832, and it was completed exactly three years later at a cost of a little over $142,000. It still carries passenger and freight trains.

The viaduct is off Levering Avenue in Elkridge. Picnic areas are in nearby Patapsco State Park.

Away from bridges and on to farms. I cover a few farm market stands and pick-your-own farms in Frederick County, but ◆**Cider Mill Farm and Larriland Farms** are more than that.

Historic Cider Mill Farm (1916) has organic produce, herbs, pies, honey, and other country goods from mid-September through November and mid-April through mid-May. During the apple season they offer guided tours of the cider-making process, including antique hand- and electric-press demonstrations in which children can participate and receive free cider samples. Tom Owens, the owner, says you can bring your own jug for fresh cider if you like.

Weekend activities include face painting, marble and yo-yo presentations, apple butter making, scarecrow making, storytelling, pumpkin carving (bring your own tools and a blanket), and a teddy bear contest (bring your own bear). Remember to bring your camera. A schedule of contests and activities is available.

Cider Mill Farm is open 10:00 A.M. to 6:00 P.M. It is located at 5012 Landing Road (off Montgomery Road, Route 103) Elkridge 21227; call (410) 788–9595 or 788–9596.

Larriland Farms has a pick-your-own season starting in late May or early June with strawberries and ending with a cut-your-own season for Christmas trees in December. In addition, the farm has succulent and delicious fruits and vegetables and beau-

tiful flowers. The market is in a 125-year-old post-and-beam barn.
Larriland Farms, owned and operated by the Moore family, also
offers hayrides, evening campfires, and other programs that let
city folk enjoy the pleasures of rural life.

The farm is open May through August, Monday through Friday
8:00 A.M. to 8:00 P.M. and September through October, Monday
through Friday 9:00 A.M. to 5:00 P.M. Weekend hours are Saturday
9:00 A.M. to 5:00 P.M. and Sunday 10:00 A.M. to 5:00 P.M. In December it's closed on Monday. The address is 2415 Woodbine Road,
Woodbine 21797. Larriland Farms is 3 miles south of I–70 (exit
73) on Route 94, near Lisbon. The phone number is (410)
489–7034; in season you can call (410) 442–2605 or (301)
854–6110 for a recording of what fruits and vegetables are available.

Toby's the Dinner Theatre of Columbia celebrates the
creative genius of Toby Orenstein and her dedication to fine theatrical productions. All the time she is working to entertain you,
she is working to teach her "kids" the hows and whys of show
business so they can go on to professional careers in entertainment if they wish.

Dinner at Toby's is an all-you-can-eat buffet that features prime
roast beef, steamed shrimp, fresh salad and vegetables, and a
dessert table. The most interesting aspect of Toby's is the theater, which has performances in the round. You are never far
from the action. The productions may be an outstanding Broadway show from years gone by, such as *Funny Girl;* the latest off
the Great White Way, such as *Singin' In the Rain;* or an entirely
new attraction, such as a musical version of *It's a Wonderful Life,*
which was created at Toby's and offered during the 1989 holiday
season. Other selections have included *The Pirates of Penzance,
Sunday in the Park with George,* and *Ain't Misbehavin'.*

Toby's is at South Entrance Road, one-half block east of Little
Patuxent Parkway, Columbia. The phone numbers are (410)
730–8311; (301) 596–6161 (in Washington); (410) 995–1969 (in
Baltimore); and (800) 88TOBYS (in Maryland and surrounding
states).

For additional information on Howard County, write to Karen
Justice, Executive Director, Howard County Tourism Council,
P.O. Box 9, Ellicott City 21041, or call (800) 288–TRIP (8747) or
(410) 313–1900.

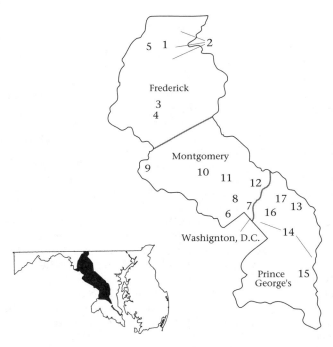

1. Apple and peach orchards
2. Covered bridges
3. *Frederick News Post*
4. Mount Olivet Cemetery
5. Campgrounds
6. Pioneer Lady statue
7. Penguin Rush Hour mural
8. Bethesda Post Office mural
9. White's Ferry

10. Roy's Place
11. Olney Theatre
12. Burn Brae Dinner Theatre
13. Greenbelt
14. Post office murals
15. DuVall Tool Collection
16. Poultry Hall of Fame
17. Patuxent Wildlife Research
    Center

GREATER WASHINGTON

Frederick, Montgomery, and Prince George's counties make up the Greater Washington area. Washington, D.C., is at the center of a huge suburban megalopolis formed by the blending of these three counties.

As a native of this area, I have received a steady stream of visitors over the years who want to tour Washington. I take them to the subway station, and the Metro Rail takes them downtown to the many Smithsonian buildings, galleries, the zoo, or anything else they want to see. The Washington Metro is as clean and safe as any subway system around and at last count was the second or third busiest subway in the country.

There are three lines running in Prince George's County, the Green, the Orange, and the Blue; and one line with two branches running in Montgomery County, the Red Line.

Green Line stations are located at Greenbelt, College Park, Prince George's Plaza, and West Hyattsville; Orange Line stations are at New Carrollton, Landover, and Cheverly; Blue Line stations are at Addison Road and Capitol Heights; and Red Line stations are at Shady Grove, Rockville, Twinbrook, White Flint, Grosvenor, Medical Center, and Bethesda going in toward Washington on the northwestern branch, and Takoma Park, Silver Spring, Forest Glen, and Wheaton coming out the more northerly route.

Trains run 5:30 A.M. to midnight on weekdays, 8:00 A.M. to midnight on Saturday, and 10:00 A.M. to midnight on Sunday. Trains run about every five to fifteen minutes, depending on the time of day. Fares are based on time and distance, with rush hour (5:30 to 9:30 A.M. and 3:00 to 7:00 P.M., weekdays) costing more than off-peak times. For a bicycle permit, call (202) 962–1116. For general information about Metro Rail and Metro Bus (such as how to get from your door to your destination), call (202) 637–7000. This number is operational from 6:00 A.M. to 11:30 P.M. daily.

Of course, this book is designed for people who are interested in seeing sights other than those along the subway routes. In the Greater Washington area you will find orchards, covered bridges, historic cemeteries, campgrounds, murals, a ferry, places to eat and to be entertained, old farm tools, and a museum dedicated to poultry, among other things.

FREDERICK COUNTY

Frederick County is renowned in certain circles for the antiques shops in New Market and Frederick, the restored train depot and museum at Brunswick, the Barbara Fritchie and Roger B. Taney homes, wineries and orchards, the Catoctin Mountains (where Camp David, the presidential retreat, is located), the Grotto of Lourdes and the St. Elizabeth Ann Seton Shrine, the Lily Pons Water Gardens, Governor Thomas Johnson's Rose Hill Manor and Schifferstadt, many churches and steeples, and, of course, that picturesque stopping point, Sugar Loaf Mountain. Still, there are other treasures here, in this, the largest county in the state.

Driving through, on interstate or back roads and particularly along Route 15, you are sure to notice the hundreds of acres of ❖ **apple and peach orchards.** The fruits of their labors are sold to the public, along with preserves, jams, country crafts, and candy. Four of these orchards deserve some notice; all are located adjacent to or just off Route 15.

Catoctin Mountain Orchard is known for its diversity and quality of all types of berries, soft fruits, apples, and vegetables. Cortland, Red and Golden Delicious, Stayman, York, and Ida Red apples are available in autumn. On weekends, however, the supply is not always sufficient for the demand; they suggest you call early in the day to reserve your fruit. You can pick your own blackberries, black raspberries, sour and sweet cherries, and strawberries, but call ahead for picking days and hours. Catoctin Mountain Orchard also offers preserved fruit and jam, packed in appealing, reusable containers. The orchard is open daily July 1 through January, and Friday, Saturday, and Sunday from January through April. It is closed May 1 through mid-July. The orchard is on Route 15, North Franklinville Road, and the mailing address is 15307 Kelbaugh Road, Thurmont 21788. Call (301) 271–2737.

Bell Hill Farm Market and Orchard is a hundred-acre farm, and the family-run fruit stand sits by a pre–Civil War home and stone springhouse. The McKissick family orchard features the tradi-tional Red and Yellow Delicious and Stayman apples, as well as some older varieties, including Grimes Golden, York, Jonathan, and Winesap. In season you can buy peaches, plums, pears, nec-tarines, watermelons, cantaloupes, raspberries, corn, beans, cucumbers, potatoes, and other produce. Bell Hill Farm is 1½ miles north of Thurmont on Route 15 and is open daily from 9:00 A.M. to 5:00 P.M. Call (301) 271–7264.

Pryor's Orchard has a modern storage facility housed in a rustic barn-type market, complete with racks of antlers and an antique cider press. Pryor's seventy-three-acre orchard is one of the oldest in the Thurmont area and a favorite of local canning enthusiasts. Pryor's is noted for its many varieties of peaches, summer and fall apples, and pears. You can pick your own blueberries and sour and sweet cherries. The orchard is closed in the winter. It is ½ mile west of Thurmont on Pryor's Road (take a left off Route 77). Call (301) 271–2693.

Scenic View Orchard has a fine selection of produce, including peaches, plums, nectarines, pears, apples (and cider), melons, sweet corn, green beans, and other vegetables. It is open daily 10.00 A.M. to 6:00 P.M. July 15 through November 1. It's located 5 miles north of Thurmont on Route 550 at 16239 Sabillasville Road, Sabillasville 21780; (301) 271–2149.

You can buy fresh fruits and vegetables or pick your own at some sixty or seventy farms and orchards in fourteen counties across the state, from Anne Arundel to Washington. Write to Marketing Resource and Development Group, Maryland Department of Agriculture, Annapolis 21401, for a copy of the current "Pick Your Own and Direct Farm Markets in Maryland" brochure. Or stop by a library or county extension office to pick up a copy.

There are three ◆ covered bridges in Frederick County. The first is **Loy's Station,** for which there is bad news and good news. It fell victim to an arsonist in the early 1990s, but restoration is now complete. This 1850 bridge crosses Owens Creek and is surrounded by a five-and-a-half–acre park. It's located on Old Frederick Road, off Route 77, about 3 miles from Thurmont.

Roddy Road Covered Bridge (1856), near Thurmont, is considered the best looking of the state's remaining bridges by covered-bridge fans. It is a single span, about 40 feet long, with a 13⅔-foot roadway. It is a fine example of basic king-post truss design, though steel stringers were installed later. Surrounding the bridge, which crosses Owens Creek, is a seventy-acre natural area for picnicking and gentle afternoon outings.

The **Utica Covered Bridge** is the largest of the three. Built in 1850, it was moved in 1889 and has been structurally reinforced with concrete piers and steel beam supports. The bridge crossed the Monocacy River until a summer flood in 1889 lifted the span from its abutments and placed it down on the river several yards away. Instead of replacing the still-intact bridge on its supports, it was dismantled, moved, and reassembled over Fishing Creek at Utica Mills. The bridge is located on Utica Road off Old Frederick Road, which is off Route 15.

Thurmont originally was called Mechanicstown because Jacob Weller, a mechanic of German descent, settled here with his family in 1751. When President Eisenhower suggested that cities take on "sister" cities in foreign countries, local newspaper editor George Wyerman decided his town should have a sister city. Because of its German background, Thurmont selected the German town of Stelzenberg, which is geographically similar to Thurmont and from which many Thurmont settlers had emigrated. In July 1988, twenty-five West Germans came to visit and started the citizens of Thurmont talking about an exchange program with Germany.

Thurmont is not only the gateway to the mountains but also the gateway to Camp David, which was originally called High Catoctin and was one of three camps built by the Civilian Conservation Corps during the Depression. The other two camps, still in existence, are Misty Mount, used for group camping, and Greentop, used by the Baltimore League of the Handicapped since 1937. The camp buildings were constructed from local timber.

High Catoctin was renamed Shangri La by Franklin Delano Roosevelt, and then renamed Camp David by Dwight D. Eisenhower. You cannot visit Camp David, but you may be able to drive by Misty Mount or Greentop to see the basic architectural style of Camp David before its presidential changes occurred.

Between Thurmont and Frederick is the old **Catoctin Furnace.** For 125 years this was a prosperous iron-making community. Started by a group of men that included the future first governor of Maryland, Thomas Johnson, the stack went into blast in 1776 to produce pig iron, tools, and household items, including the popular ten-plate stove. Bombshells for 10-inch mortars were produced toward the end of the Revolutionary War.

By the mid-eighteenth century, the owner of the furnace had eighty houses for his workers, a sawmill, gristmill, company store, farms, ore railroad, three furnace stacks (including an anthracite coal stack), and more than 11,000 acres of land.

By 1903 the furnace ceased to operate, although ore was taken out of this area until 1912. What is left on the northern side of this "company town" is the furnace and an early nineteenth-century double log house, which is preserved by the Catoctin Furnace Historical Society and used as a museum and interpretive center.

For additional information write to the Catoctin Furnace Historical Society, Thurmont 21788, or call Cunningham Falls State Park, (301) 271–7574. The furnace, remaining houses in Catoctin Village, and Harriet Chapel can be seen along Route 806, on the east side of Route 15, about 12 miles north of Frederick.

The ✦*Frederick News Post* offers day and night tours through the newspaper office for adults and children as young as four or five. The tour lasts about forty-five minutes and goes through the editorial, advertising, circulation, and press rooms, and it provides an explanation about how a paper is written and printed. At night Ed Waters gives the tours; during the day it is Mike Powell and Karen James who do the honors. They like to have about two weeks' notice before tours and prefer not more than twenty to a group.

You might think that the building does not seem to connect properly in the middle, and you would be right. Stand back from the front facade and notice that the front door has been filled in; this used to be a trolley barn, and the trolleys would go through the middle of the buildings on either side of this central portion. You can tell from the way the floor goes up and down with almost no rhyme or reason that it was put together after the fact. Sorry, but the trolley tracks have been removed.

For tour reservations or information, contact the *Frederick News Post,* 200 East Patrick Street, Frederick 21701, (301–662–1177).

A word about churches in Frederick. There are ten of note and one synagogue, and their histories and architectural styles date from the colonial, revolutionary, and Civil War eras. Tours are available during the year, and a brochure is available from the Frederick Tourism Council that details the history of each house of worship. A special time for all the houses of worship is the Candlelight Tour held in December, when each is decorated for the holiday, and hosts are on hand to greet visitors and answer questions. Special music and presentations are provided at various churches throughout the evening and free parking is available. Hospitality rooms are located at a number of places, and the one at Trunk Hall in the Evangelical Lutheran Church is handicapped accessible.

Many prominent Marylanders now reside in ❖**Mount Olivet Cemetery,** including Francis Scott Key, Barbara Fritchie, and Governor Thomas Johnson, along with veterans of the American Revolution, the Civil War (more than 800 Confederate soldiers), and World War II, as well as more than 25,000 other people.

A statue of Key stands over 9 feet tall on a monument that is 16 feet high and 45 feet around; you can't miss the statue because it welcomes you at the main entrance. The United States flag standing by him flies twenty-four hours a day in honor of his writing the words to "The Star-Spangled Banner." Much of the money collected for the $25,000 monument was donated in dimes and dollars by people all over the country.

Little green-and-white signs direct you to the graves of Governor Johnson and Barbara Fritchie, who are across the road from each other. Johnson was a Revolutionary War patriot, born in Frederick County in 1732 (the same year as George Washington), and was a prominent member of the Continental Congress. He was the first governor of the State of Maryland and associate justice of the United States Supreme Court.

Fritchie was made immortal by John Greenleaf Whittier's poem about her bravery against General Stonewall Jackson, when she flew the Union flag and dared soldiers to "Shoot if you must, this old gray head, but spare your country's flag." A monument of Maryland granite with the Whittier poem on a bronze tablet was unveiled on September 9, 1914.

The cemetery is considered one of the most beautiful and distinguished in this part of the country. The address is Mount Olivet Cemetery, South Broadway, Frederick 21701.

There are numerous ❖**campgrounds** where you can spend a night or two, and Frederick is close enough to Washington and Baltimore to be used as a base, if you wish.

One of the better-known private campgrounds is Crow's Nest Lodge Campground, owned and operated by Ned and Renna Haynes. It has 110 campsites located along Big Hunting Creek, a mountain trout stream that flows through the Catoctin Mountains. Each spacious campsite is designed to accommodate a large tent, tent trailer, or travel trailer. Most of the sites are shaded, and many have water and electricity.

59

At the campground you can enjoy a spring-fed, freshwater pond for swimming and wading; 10 miles of scenic foot trails that wind through the Catoctin Mountain park; fishing; nature study; and a half-dozen action sports. Pets are welcome, as long as they are on a leash at all times. The address is Crow's Nest Lodge Campground, P.O. Box 145, Thurmont 21788. Call (301) 271–7632.

As mentioned in the Washington County section, several creative people there have banded together to create the Valley Craft Network. One of the members is Susan Hanson of **Catoctin Pottery,** the only network member in Frederick County.

Susan makes handmade stoneware and porcelain in an 1810 water-powered gristmill on Catoctin Creek. Lewis Mill is a prime example of the adaptive use of a historic structure; the mill is meticulously reconstructed and houses a modern living space, studio, and retail showroom. Preservation of the environment is demonstrated by the use of solar heat and a waterless composting toilet.

In the studio showroom are works in clay, such as tableware, table and swag lamps, ceramic art, wall plaques, and tiles. Commissions are accepted.

Catoctin Pottery is open Monday through Saturday, 10:00 A.M. to 5:00 P.M., and is located on Poffenberger Road, off Old Middletown Road, Jefferson 21755, (301–731–4274).

For additional tourism information, write to the Executive Director, Tourism Council of Frederick County, 19 East Church Street, Frederick 21701, or call (301) 663–8687 or (800) 999–3613.

MONTGOMERY COUNTY

Longtime area residents (anyone who's been here for more than fifteen years) will remember the awkward, sprawling image of the Bethesda intersection of Wisconsin Avenue, Old Georgetown Road, and East-West Highway. Personally, I remember it from when we used to hang out at the Hot Shoppes restaurant on Saturdays after high school football games between archrivals Montgomery Blair and Bethesda Chevy Chase. (Go, Blazers!)

The presence at this intersection of the ◆**Pioneer Lady statue,** or Madonna of the Trail, statue symbolizes the importance of these roads even in their early days. Harry Truman dedicated the statue on April 19, 1949, in honor of the pioneer spirit and the

National Pike, which connected the country from this spot on the East Coast to the town of Upland, California, on the West Coast. This was the twelfth of twelve statues to be installed. The other statues were erected (chronologically) in Springfield, Ohio; Wheeling, West Virginia; Council Grove, Kansas; Lexington, Missouri; Lamar, Colorado; Albuquerque, New Mexico; Springerville, Arizona; Vandalia, Illinois; Richmond, Indiana; Washington, Pennsylvania; and Upland, California.

The memorial (which faces east, whereas most of the other statues face west) is dedicated to the pioneer mothers of the covered-wagon days. The engraving reads: OVER THIS HIGHWAY MARCHED THE ARMY OF MAJOR GENERAL EDWARD BRADDOCK, APRIL 14, 1755, ON ITS WAY TO FORT DUQUESNE, AND [THIS IS] THE FIRST MILITARY ROAD IN AMERICA, BEGINNING AT ROCK CREEK AND POTOMAC RIVER, GEORGETOWN, MARYLAND, LEADING OUR PIONEERS ACROSS THE CONTINENT TO THE PACIFIC. The Pioneer Lady statue is located between the post office and the Hyatt Regency Hotel at the corner of Wisconsin Avenue, East-West Highway, and Old Georgetown Road in Bethesda.

When the statue was installed in 1986, after years in storage due to subway and hotel construction, it was the first in a collection of perhaps twenty-five commissioned works by visual artists to be installed along Bethesda's streets. Known as the Bethesda Urban District, this area has more than 170 restaurants, from traditional to trendy, from down-home to deluxe. One of these is the Benihana in the Airrights Building, which is one of the oldest restaurants in the district and, when it opened in 1974, was only the sixteenth in the Benihana chain.

Downtown Silver Spring also has changed drastically and will continue to do so as the metro influences work and travel patterns. Even if you do not use the metro system to travel into Washington, stop by the Silver Spring station.

A mural, 100 feet long and 8 feet high, was installed as part of the MetroArt I arts project (see also Prince George's County). Created by Sally Callmer of Bethesda, who previously was a miniaturist, the ◆Penguin Rush Hour Mural was meant as a temporary installation but has become such an integral part of the community that the Montgomery County Department of Transportation has purchased the twenty-five panels as a permanent fixture. The mural brings life to a previously drab area, and because of the lighting, it is the single brightest point in that downtown area. The idea for the penguin signs advocating ride sharing and use of the metro came from this mural.

Montgomery's Forest Glen metro station, which is nearly 200 feet below ground level, is the deepest in the system and maybe in the world. The Wheaton escalator, at more than 228 feet, is the metro system's longest escalator.

While you are in Silver Spring, drive by the **Silver Spring Acorn.** It is easy to spot this little park, located near the spring from which the area received its name, with its gazebo shaped by pillars and a "hat" with the configuration of an acorn. Benches are provided for a lunch break or a moment of rest. Francis Preston Blair—a wealthy and prominent eighteenth-century landowner, power broker, newspaper owner, and member of President Jackson's Kitchen Cabinet—and his daughter were out riding one day when they found this spring. The sunlight reflecting off the sand or mica in the bottom made the minerals look like silver, and thus was born the name of his estate and the area, Silver Spring.

In 1942 the park was acquired by a local citizens group, and it was restored in 1955. Incidentally, the area, which is not incorporated, is called Silver Spring, not "springs," as in the Florida town. The Silver Spring Acorn is on Newell Road at the intersection of East-West Highway and Blair Mill Road, 1 block south of Georgia Avenue (across the street from the Canada Dry bottling plant).

Near the Takoma Park metro station are a number of boutiques, including Arise for ethnic and contemporary fashions; an agreeable bakery called Everyday Gourmet; Kaz department store, which is billed as the smallest department store in the world; and Now & Then, which specializes in cotton basics for women and children as well as restyled military and vintage items "for the whimsical, wacky and wearable."

On Saturdays from spring-to-fall, a block of Laurel Avenue is closed to vehicular traffic and becomes a farmer's market, which has people nearly clogging the subway system for early-morning selections. For more information write to Historic Takoma, P.O. Box 5781, Takoma Park 20912, or call (301) 585–3542.

Another farmer's market is located in Bethesda, 2 or 3 blocks from the above-mentioned Pioneer Lady statue. This is the **Montgomery Farm Woman's Cooperative Market,** which is open on Wednesday and Saturday throughout the year.

This market was started during the Depression, with its first

Silver Spring Acorn

sale date set for February 4, 1932. A second sale was held on April 20, and it became so popular that they began a traditional Wednesday and Saturday selling date. You can stop by the market and find all manner of foods—including Pennsylvania Dutch double baked ham and baked goods—and even some rocking chairs and other craft items, particularly during the winter. Our favorite stall is the Marquez Farm Stand in the back left-hand corner, as you walk in from Wisconsin Avenue, where Rick and Chun II Marquez, and sometimes their daughter, sell the most delectable pies, cakes, scones, Baltimore cheese breads, quiches, tarts, muffins, all-beef summer sausage, bratwurst, German salami, nitrite-free bacon, and the list goes on. You can reach the Marquez family at (301) 530–9098.

The Montgomery Farm Woman's Market, at 7155 Wisconsin Avenue, Bethesda 20814, is open Wednesday and Saturday 7:00 A.M. to 2:00 P.M.

Another view of the market is in the ◆ **Bethesda Post Office mural** painted by Robert Gates in 1939. This definitely represents a Montgomery County tradition, unlike the stereotypical transportation scene painted in the Towson Post Office. The Bethesda mural was restored in 1967 with funds provided by the Montgomery Farm Woman's Cooperative Market. The post office is at 7400 Wisconsin Avenue, Bethesda 20814.

Two other post office buildings in the area have murals. One is in Silver Spring and was painted in 1937 by Nicolai Cikovsky (of the Towson transportation mural incident); it's called "The Old Tavern," reflecting life in the area during and after the antebellum period. The Old Post Office Building is at 8412 Georgia Avenue, Silver Spring 20901.

The other mural was done by New York artist Judson Smith in 1940 and is of "Sugar Loaf Mountain." Supposedly, it was painted from the porch of an estate called Inverness, which was built in 1818 by Benjamin White. The view includes fields and farm buildings, and the mural hangs over the wall where the lock boxes used to be located. Rockville Post Office is at 2 West Montgomery Avenue, Rockville 20850.

Speaking of the White family, ◆ **White's Ferry** is the only remaining ferry system on the Potomac River, connecting White's Ferry, Maryland, to Leesburg, Virginia. It probably is more important these days than when it began operation in

Montgomery Farm Woman's Cooperative Market

1828, for it is the only river crossing between the American Legion Bridge on the Washington (or Capital) Beltway to the south and east, and the Point of Rocks bridge to the north and west. Regular commuters and tourists can easily tell when there is a major backup on the Beltway because these back-country roads become filled with drivers escaping the jam.

The ferry *General Jubal Early* (named for a Confederate leader) runs the 1,000-foot crossing on a cable propelled by a diesel tug in about three minutes. It can hold fifteen cars and operates all year, weather and river conditions permitting, on a demand basis. A country store selling sundries and souvenirs is open on the Maryland side from spring through fall. The ferry is off Route 107. Call (301) 394–5200 for information.

Just up the ramp from White's Ferry landing is the ditch that was once the Chesapeake & Ohio Canal and is now the longest and thinnest National Historical Park in the country, narrowing to less than 50 feet at one point. There was a time when there were twenty trading posts along the 185-mile canal, which ran from Cumberland to Washington, D.C., roughly paralleling the Potomac River.

In 1988 conservationists spent three months clearing away foliage and found the 150-foot foundation of a nineteenth-century depot and granary. From the Civil War until 1924, canal boats headed down to Washington, D.C., where they would tie up to a three-story wooden storage building called the Granary to load up with grain from area farms. In the sixty years since the canal closed, the Granary and canal have been neglected and overgrown by trees and shrubbery.

When you tell someone you're going to ◆ **Roy's Place,** they think you're talking about that old cowboy movie star. But this Roy's Place is in Gaithersburg, and it is far from fast food and fast eating. In fact, the menu tells you that if you are in a hurry, go someplace else. No, it is not fine dining. It is just sandwiches, and more sandwiches—some of the weirdest sandwiches you've ever imagined.

How would you like a sandwich with roast beef, fried oysters, and a side serving of tartar sauce? Would you prefer provolone cheese, anchovies, blue cheese dressing, onions, and lettuce? Or would you like something else? The menu features some 170 different sandwiches, or you can start at the front page with a salad selection and skip to the back page for a simple hamburger, if you do not feel like reading the equivalent of a novella before you eat. Roy's has been open since 1971, and several local and national celebrities have had sandwiches named after them. The decor is just as interesting and offbeat as the menu, with posters, old advertisements, and a sign by the skylight that says THIS WAY OUT. Roy's Place is at 2 East Diamond Avenue, Gaithersburg (301–948–5548). Hours are Monday through Thursday 11:00 A.M. to 11:00 P.M., Friday and Saturday 11:00 A.M. to midnight, and Sunday 12:00 noon to 11:00 P.M. No reservations are accepted.

The ❖ **Olney Theatre** opened in 1942 as a stop on the summer "straw hat" circuit, closed because of the war, and then reopened in 1946 with Helen Hayes starring in *Good Housekeeping*. Other luminaries who have graced its stage include Tallulah Bankhead, Gloria Swanson, and Bea Lillie. The late Reverend Gilbert Hartke, head of Catholic University's drama department, took over the management in 1953, providing exposure for his students as well as Carol Channing, John McGiver, and Frances Sternhagen. Bill Graham is now managing director and James D. Waring is artistic director.

Also known as the State Summer Theatre of Maryland, Olney Theatre started a new tradition in 1989 with the annual production of *The Butterfingers Angel, Mary & Joseph, Herod the Nut, and the Slaughter of 12 Hit Carols in a Pear Tree,* a Christmas entertainment by noted playwright William Gibson. The theater also is known for the elected officials it attracts, particularly on opening night, both to see the outstanding presentations and to be seen.

The Victorian farmhouse (circa 1880) next door is the Actors' Residence, where housing is provided for the cast in season. Actually two casts stay there at one time, one for the show in production and one for the show in rehearsal. On opening night post-performance festivities take place here.

The mailing address for Olney Theatre is P.O. Box 550, 2001 Route 108, Olney 20832; the phone number is (301) 924–3400.

After a day of sightseeing, you can stop by the ❖ **Burn Brae Dinner Theatre** in Burtonsville. Burn Brae was the first dinner theater in the Washington area (opened in 1968), and it has continued to provide outstanding entertainment. At times it presents a full-blown production with a huge cast, such as *Joseph and the Amazing Technicolor Dreamcoat* or *Evita,* and at other times it shows small, intimate plays such as *I Do! I Do!* There may even be a preshow tabletop magician or a weekly children's magic show.

With each show there is a menu change, but a typical buffet might consist of seventeen items, including salad, fish, roast beef, honey-basted Virginia ham, pasta primavera, chicken, meatballs, hot vegetables, homemade bread and muffins, and desserts. When Burn Brae opened in an unused dressing room of a community pool in 1968, little did Bernie Levin and John Kinnamon realize they were starting a terrific tradition. At one time the Washington area was the home of the largest number of dinner theaters in the country. Because there were so many of them, they fostered a group of performers who knew they would receive excellent training as well as be seen by the many talent scouts who came through this area.

Burn Brae Dinner Theatre is at 15029 Blackburn Road, Burtonsville 20866; call (301) 792–0290 or 384–5800.

For additional tourism information, write to Johnnie Lingebach, Visitor Center Manager, Conference & Visitors Bureau of Montgomery County, MD Inc., 12900 Middlebrook Road, Suite 1400, Germantown 20874, or call (301) 428–9702 or (800) 925–0880.

PRINCE GEORGE'S COUNTY

People hear more about Prince George's County in the news than they realize. A sports event is broadcast from the USAir Arena in Largo; a marriage is performed on the old wooden roller coaster at the Adventure World theme park outside Kettering; someone inquires into the status of the *Enola Gay* restoration at the Paul E. Garber Facility in Silver Hill (part of the National Air and Space Museum of the Smithsonian Institution); space flight information is reported from the Goddard Space Flight Center (and Museum) in Greenbelt, the hub of all NASA tracking activities; or the president arrives at Andrews Air Force Base, the home base for Air Force One. Of course, Prince George's County is rarely mentioned, but all of this commerce, sport, and history is taking place here on a day-to-day basis.

Prince George's County is a place of "firsts" and "lasts." In the latter category is the Bladensburg Dueling Grounds, a small, wooden glen in the northeastern corner of Fort Lincoln Cemetery, adjacent to Colmar Manor. It was a court of last resort for nearly fifty years for offended gentlemen and politicians, who faced each other at ten paces with pistols and muskets. As noted on the historical marker placed by the Maryland–National Capital Park and Planning Commission:

> One of the most famous was that between Commodores Stephen Decatur and James Barron which was settled here on March 22, 1820. Commodore Decatur, who had gained fame as the conqueror of the Barbary pirates, was fatally wounded by his antagonist. Although Congress passed an anti-dueling law in 1839, duels continued here until just before the Civil War.

The dueling grounds are in Anacostia River Park and near the intersection of Bladensburg Road and Thirty-eighth Avenue in Bladensburg. Also at Anacostia River Park is the Maryland–National Capital Park and Planning Commission Interpretive Center at the site of the old Bladensburg Marina.

College Park Airport is where the first military training in a military-owned airplane took place in October 1909. The plane was designed by Orville and Wilbur Wright. College Park claims to be the "world's oldest continually operated airport," and today it is the only operating airport within the Capital Beltway. Pilots say they get a kick out of flying from the same airfield that the Wright Brothers used eighty some years ago. Budding aviators are sure to enjoy the College Park Airport museum. It's free and is open from 11:00 A.M. to 3:00 P.M. Wednesday through Friday and 11:00 A.M. to 5:00 P.M. Saturday and Sunday. Call (301) 864–1530.

To those who think planned cities are new to the seventies or eighties, meet ✦ **Greenbelt,** a "first" in the arena of planned cities that was started in the thirties. From its inception, Greenbelt had a sense of history about it. It has been chronicled, cataloged, dissected, scrutinized, and studied many times over in thorough detail. Although its "greenbelt" has been gnawed away a little and the town is surrounded by townhouse communities for Washington commuters, you still can see the core of the town, its art deco architecture, and its attempts to retain its identity.

Greenbelt is one of three planned greenbelt towns that were to be satellite towns on the edge of larger urban cores (the other two are Greenhills, Ohio, and Greendale, Wisconsin, outside of Cincinnati and Milwaukee, respectively). The town was built around an inner core, allowing residents to walk everywhere they had to go on pedestrian paths so that people on foot would not have to intermingle with cars.

The town was superorganized and highly democratic, and residents met to discuss everything. (In fact, at one point they met to declare a moratorium on meetings.)

For a more thorough explanation and visual interpretation, stop by the Greenbelt Museum on Sunday between 1:00 and 5:00 P.M. There's no admission charge. The museum is located at 10 B Crescent Road. Call (301) 474–1936.

Greenbelt is at the northwest corner of the intersection of the Baltimore-Washington Parkway (I–295) and the Capital Beltway (I–495).

Special library collections abound in Prince George's County. The Greenbelt Library has the Tugwell Room. As the Belair Estate in Bowie claimed to be the "Cradle of American Racing," it seems entirely appropriate that the Bowie Library has the Selima Room, with its extensive collection of horse-racing records and materials. Selima was one of the original mares who started the bloodline that flows in almost every racehorse in this country.

Other special collections in the Prince George's County library system include the Sojourner Truth Room in the Oxon Hill branch, the Kerlan Room children's collection in the Hyattsville branch, and the Documents Library in the County Administration Building in Upper Marlboro, which appears to have every document pertaining to Prince George's County that was ever printed or penned.

The performing and visual arts are important in this county, which is highly populated with Washington and Baltimore commuters. The Montpelier Center in Laurel is noted for its visual arts. Visual and performing arts options at the University of Maryland in College Park are nearly limitless, and the annual International Piano Competition always draws an extraordinary crowd.

Also, after four years of planning and building, the county officially opened the doors to a fine arts facility at **Harmony Hall Regional Center** in September 1989. Responding to the county's need for a professional music space and additional visual arts programs in the southern portion of the county, the vacant Harmony Hall Elementary School was renovated to include the 210-seat John Addison Concert Hall, a lobby, and a gallery space. An infrared radio system was included to assist the hearing impaired. The school's former garden atrium and two classrooms were removed for the concert hall and lobby, and an interior wall between two other adjacent classrooms was removed to allow for a large exhibition space on the building's ground floor. On the second floor two more classrooms were combined to provide for a professional dance studio. For information on upcoming programs and exhibits, write to the Harmony Hall Regional Center, 10701 Livingston Road, Fort Washington 20744, or call (301) 292–8331.

Several years ago the arts organizations of Prince George's and Montgomery counties in Maryland, northern Virginia, and Washington, D.C., agreed to promote a **MetroArts** contest for public art to be displayed in subway stations throughout the system. It was very successful, and a number of artists had works displayed at several metro stations, such as New Carrollton, for a year. A second contest, this one with prize money totalling $100,000, has been held. New Carrollton again has been selected to have a three-dimensional artwork display, which will be on display for two years. (See also the Montgomery County section for details on the Silver Spring metro station mural, which has been purchased for permanent installation.)

If you like murals as much as I do, you will be curious about Prince George's County's ❖ **post office murals.** The one in Laurel of the "Mail Coach at Laurel," painted by Mitchell Jamieson in 1939, reportedly was taken down during a General Services Administration restoration of the building and has not been returned.

Eugene Kingman, a noted muralist, painter, and museum director, created the five panels in the Hyattsville Post Office in 1938, jointly entitled "Hyattsville Countryside." He was born in 1909, attended Yale University College of Fine Arts, and received an honorary Ph.D. from Creighton University. His work is in the Library of Congress collection and at the Philbrook in Tulsa, Oklahoma, among many other places. He also created post office murals in Wyoming and Rhode Island and in the lobby of the New York Times Building in New York City.

The Hyattsville murals depict the working man in heroic proportions. They reflect the remains of the agricultural and pastoral quality of the Hyattsville lifestyle that still existed in 1937 when Kingman used such muralist techniques as stylized horses, foreshortening, and a decorative cornstalk border.

71

The Hyattsville Post Office is at 4325 Gallatin Street, Hyattsville 20781. Call (301) 669–8905.

Understanding that Prince George's County was and still is a very agrarian county, you will appreciate the work of W. Henry DuVall. A lifelong Prince Georgean, DuVall had the foresight to save tools from the nineteenth century, whether it was a scythe, froe, niddy-noddy, can opener, carpenter's plane, or foot-operated dental drill. This was the beginning of the ✦ **DuVall Tool Collection.** There is even a white building block that is blackened on one side, which apparently was obtained during a nineteenth-century architectural revision of the White House. The dark stains are said to be soot from the burning of the building during the War of 1812.

The Maryland National Capital Park and Planning Commission had the foresight to buy the agglomeration so that it would not be lost to the twentieth or twenty-first century. DuVall's collection, which he started in the 1930s, had more than 1,200 items by the time he died in 1979. More tools are accepted, so if you have something tucked away in your attic or out in the garage someplace—particularly if it is unique to Southern Maryland history—donate it here instead of to the dump.

You can return to yesteryear by viewing the DuVall Tool Collection, located in the Patuxent River Park, Sunday from 1:00 to 4:00 P.M. and by appointment. The address is 16000 Croom Airport Road, Upper Marlboro 20772. Call (301) 672–6074.

Poultry is a big part of the eastern and not the western shore's economy, so it might not make sense that there is a ✦ **Poultry Hall of Fame** in Beltsville. It was here, however, that the big-breasted Beltsville turkey you enjoy so much at Thanksgiving was created; thus its originator, Dr. T. C. Byerly, is honored here. Five poultry greats are inducted into this society every year.

Actually, Beltsville is the Department of Agriculture's largest research center, and the tour offered there is fascinating. A visitor's center, in Building 186 (East), the Log Lodge, is open daily from 9:00 A.M. to 4:00 P.M. Guided tours are available by appointment. Call (301) 504–9403. The mailing address is United States Department of Agriculture, National Agriculture Library, Second Floor, 10301 Baltimore-Washington Boulevard, Beltsville 20705. There is no admission charge.

There is other wildlife occupying the minds of specialists in Prince George's County. Situated on 4,700 acres, the ✦ **Patuxent**

Wildlife Research Center specializes in research on endangered species, migratory birds, and environmental contaminants. Established in 1839 as America's first national wildlife experiment station, the center is charged with protecting and conserving the nation's wildlife and natural habitats through research and critical debate. Throughout the years, the center has been involved in history-making discoveries, including the detrimental effects of DDT. Rachel Carson did most of her research here for her book *Silent Spring*.

Currently the center is working to save the endangered whooping crane, California condor, Mississippi sandhill crane, and masked bobwhite. It has completed successfully a program of repopulating America's proud symbol, the bald eagle. Scientists from more than fifteen countries conduct research at the center on a regular basis.

Patuxent is the largest wildlife research center in the world, and it is an exciting place to learn about global concerns, be a field researcher and travel through the five full-scale habitat areas, view acres of natural wildlife habitat, and see dramatic dioramas of wildlife. Tram tours of the surrounding woods and lakes to learn about wildlife management are offered during the summer at 10:30 and 11:30 A.M. and 12:30 and 1:30 P.M. Prices are $1.00 for students and $2.00 for adults. Groups may schedule tram tours. A gift shop offers a variety of environmental books, gifts, and educational materials.

The Center and the National Fund for the Patuxent Wildlife Research Center were featured on a December 1989 *CBS Sunday Morning* with Charles Kuralt. The fund is a special committee of the Prince George's County Parks and Recreation Foundation, Inc., which facilitates a public/private partnership to raise funds on a national basis for the multimillion dollar National Wildlife Visitor Center.

The visitor's center will have a mission to "educate the public, especially students, about wildlife conservation from a global perspective." The research center is located off Powder Mill Road, 2 miles east of the Baltimore/Washington Parkway. The mailing address is 10901 Scarlet Tanager Loop, Laurel 20708-4027. Call Nell Baldachinno (301–498–0331 or –0300) at least several days in advance to arrange a tour.

The Chesapeake Bay area is noted for its seafood, and one of

73

the better places to enjoy it—on the half shell, in crab cakes, or as part of a seafood platter—is at the **Bay n Surf** restaurant. This has been an institution of fine food since Roxanne and Patrick Edelmann opened it in 1965. The community has grown up and changed around it, but Bay n Surf retains that friendly "Cheers" atmosphere. Of course, there are nonseafood options. Bay n Surf is located at 14411 Baltimore Avenue (US Route 1), Laurel. Call (301) 776–7021.

Near the USAir Arena and the new Redskins stadium is the flagship restaurant **BET Soundstage,** from BET Holdings, Inc., the first and only cable network for the African-American community. This restaurant features a dynamic sensory experience through taped performances and a state-of-the-art multimedia display of video and music. Music celebrities, sports figures, artists, and business professionals provide a mix of the famous and the familiar among its clientele. A gift shop, filled with the latest BET branded merchandise, including T-shirts, jackets, and caps, is on the premises.

BET Soundstage is located at 4315 Lottsford Court, Landover, near Lottsford Road and Route 202.

Just south of Upper Marlboro, the county seat, is the old-turned-to-new Prince George's Equestrian Center and the newer Showplace Arena. Once a functional horse racetrack, it was closed and converted to fringe parking for county employees before it was reborn as an architectural masterpiece and the home of the annual county fair, concerts, and other special events. There are even a few days of horse racing now and then. You'll find the center and arena at the intersection of Routes 301 and 4. Call (301) 952–4740.

Last, but not least, is the covered bridge in Bowie. It's located at the Bowie Race Course, which is now an equestrian center rather than a racetrack. Alas, the bridge is used for horses to move from the stables to the track for their workouts, not for people or cars. It is almost brand new—construction was completed in 1988—making it perhaps the only covered bridge to have been built in this country in decades.

For additional information about Prince George's County, from events to lodgings, contact Matt Neitzey and his staff at the Prince George's County Conference and Visitors Bureau, 9475 Lottsford Road, Suite 130, Landover 20785. Call (301) 925–8300.

SOUTHERN MARYLAND

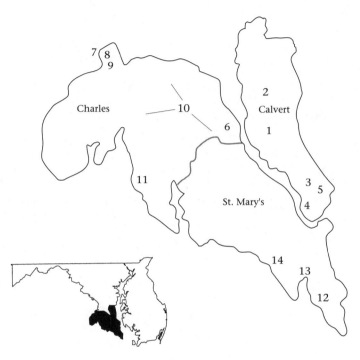

1. Country Peddler of Calvert County
2. The Wright Touch
3. Vera's White Sands
4. Calvert Marine Museum and Drum Point Lighthouse
5. Flag Ponds Nature Park
6. Benedict
7. Marshall Hall

8. Mount Carmel Monastery
9. Friendship House
10. Tobacco auctions
11. Pope's Creek
12. Freedom of Conscience Statue
13. Toddy Hall Pottery
14. Piney Point Lighthouse Museum and Park

SOUTHERN MARYLAND

Parts of Charles, Calvert (pronounced "Cawlvert" or "Calvit" by the locals), and St. Mary's counties probably have changed more because of avulsion and accretion than because of developmental encroachment since the first English colonists settled here in the mid-1600s.

With the more stringent wetlands restrictions recently imposed by our federal and state governments, it is possible that the Southern Maryland you see today will be the same as the one you see in ten, twenty, thirty, or more years from now.

As you drive down these roads, you will see signs of early settlements when brave men and women came seeking new lives, religious freedom, and adventure. Dozens of churches, some dating from the early eighteenth century, dot the historic landscape.

Water has made its influence felt, of course; there are many waterside communities, places to buy and eat fresh seafood, and aquatic research centers.

In Southern Maryland I looked for markets that keep a community alive, and I found several community craft centers and talented artisans. I hope you will take the time to enjoy the maritime influence and the fine and unusual dining surrounding, or perhaps surrounded by, this rich coastal area.

CALVERT COUNTY

If you like country crafts, you'll find them in Calvert County; for this is country, although it is rapidly being encroached upon by civilization. Here are two places to go where the crafts of many artisans are represented.

Nearly two dozen local crafters show their work at the ◆ **Country Peddler of Calvert County,** a showcase for local talent including Janet Richardson, whose "Paws for Thought" collection includes stuffed animals; Nan Reid's crochet and knit items; Mary Rasmussen's counted cross-stitch needlework and silhouettes; Owen Myers's canvas bags; Margaret Clark Smith's ceramics; Madie Winike's stained-glass pieces; and Virgie Finley's needlepoint. Also sold here are potpourri, homegrown loofahs, and handmade brooms from the Calvert Homestead.

The Country Peddler is behind Bowens Grocery, where you

can buy hand-cut meats, and across the street from the Bowens Garage Antique Center. The shop is open 10:00 A.M. to 5:00 P.M. Thursday, Friday, and Saturday; it is located parallel to Route 2-4, on Old Town Road, Route 524, Huntingtown 20639. Call (410) 257–3105.

Works from nationally recognized crafters can be found at ✦ **The Wright Touch,** owned and operated by sisters Sue Hill and Eve Wright. Tom Clark Woodspirits may be the biggest-selling items here, and Clark even stops by to talk with his fans. You can find handcrafted gifts, handwoven throws, country pine furniture, collectibles, decorating accessories, Christmas decorations, and Christmas curtains.

The Wright Touch is at 3150 Solomons Island Road, Route 4 southbound (turn at Gardner's Citgo station), Huntingtown 20639. Call (410) 535–5588. The shop is open Tuesday through Thursday 11:00 A.M. to 6:00 P.M., Friday and Saturday 10:00 A.M. to 6:00 P.M., and Sunday noon to 5:00 P.M. Inquire about winter holiday hours and the Christmas antique festival.

While in the neighborhood you can visit Barbara Burnett at her small Calvert Homestead barn, the "Home of the R & B Brand," which was featured on one of the home shopping networks, furthering her renown. Travel south on Route 2-4 to Sixes Road (Route 506) and drive in about 3 miles. It will be on your right at 4555 Sixes Road, Prince Frederick. Call (410) 535–3786 for hours and information.

On the way there, you will pass the **Battle Creek Cypress Swamp Sanctuary.** This is the northernmost stand of bald cypress trees in the country. There is neither Spanish moss hanging from these boughs nor southern belles in hoop skirts; instead, there is a good interpretive center and a great place for nature photography in the spring and early summer when the blooms are most profuse. Bring fast film and a tripod, because the light is heavily filtered through the canopy.

By the way, those thick, fuzzy vines climbing the trees along the boardwalk through the swamp are poison ivy, and they are just as dangerous as their cousin with the three shiny leaves if you are allergic to it. The sanctuary is on Grays Road off Sixes Road (Route 506). Call (410) 535–5327.

There are places called Hollywood and California in Maryland (both in St. Mary's County), and major motion pictures have been made in the state, but nothing equals ❖ **Vera's White Sands** restaurant. A summer pastime that should not be missed, Vera Freeman's restaurant is decorated with souvenirs from her worldwide travels.

Imagine you are Lauren Bacall, Humphrey Bogart, or Peter Lorre, or even Bob Hope, Bing Crosby, or Hedy Lamarr on the road to someplace; you would feel right at home here. What are your decorative tastes? Would you like banana trees framing the flamingo pink structure? How do you like beaded room dividers, carved elephants inlaid with ivory, giant clamshells, and leopard-skin bar stools to provide the atmosphere? Steam up the scene with a little romantic intrigue, and you do not have to travel far to find the wondrous. The view from the appropriately described picture windows and the piano overlooks historic John's Creek, off the Patuxent River. The creek is wide, and the channel depth is 14 feet. The marina has docking facilities for 100 boats (water depth at dock is 12 feet), and a dockmaster is on the premises twenty-four hours a day, year-round.

Vera's seafood specialty (bouillabaisse with shrimp, scallops, filet of fish, crab, clams, and mussels) is served in a tomato-and-wine sauce. My personal favorite is the crab cakes, light and gently broiled (you may have them fried). In June, July, and August you may have your cocktails poolside.

About 6:30 P.M. on Friday, Saturday, and Sunday evenings, you'll be diverted by live entertainment; and around 7:30 P.M. the J. Arthur Rank–style gong will be sounded as Vera makes her entrance. Vera's is a place you will long remember.

Vera's White Sands is in Lusby on White Sands Drive. The restaurant is open from May 1 through Columbus Day, Tuesday through Saturday 5:00 to 9:00 P.M. and Sunday 1:00 to 9:00 P.M. Reservations are suggested.

Continuing south or southeast on Route 2-4, you will come to Solomons, which has a visitor center that is open from spring through late fall. Across the street is the ❖ **Calvert Marine Museum and Drum Point Lighthouse,** and parking is behind the administration building.

The Calvert Marine Museum is proof that a museum can be fun, fascinating, and fact filled. This museum has grown from a seed planted by LeRoy "Pepper" Langley in 1970, and it is certainly worth a visit for a number of reasons.

The first reason is the Children's Discovery Room, where there is a pile of earth with fossils from Calvert Cliffs that you can dig in. It can be difficult and time-consuming to search for fossils at outdoor sites, but not here. One shark's tooth per person, please. This room is more fun than a bushel of crabs that has just been dusted with seasoning. Yet there is more, and you are on your own to enjoy, to be entertained, and to be educated. Even the more conventional exhibits about boating, the paleontology of Calvert Cliffs, and the estuarine biology of the Patuxent River and Chesapeake Bay are well handled.

The museum's second treasure is the **Drum Point Lighthouse,** one of the old screw-pile, cottage-style lighthouses that used to protect the adventuresome watermen of the bay. The two-story, hexagon-shaped structure was built in 1883 to mark the entrance of the Patuxent River. A crane and barge moved the stilted cottage to its current location in 1975. Take a few minutes to walk through the lighthouse (watch your head when going up and down the steps) and mentally transport yourself to the time when people lived here and tended the light. It is romantic to think of the "good old days" when there were lightkeepers, but most don't think this remote lifestyle is very attractive these days.

The third treasure is an old bugeye, the *William B. Tennison,* which takes people on cruises around the bay. This bugeye is a Chesapeake Bay sailing craft built in 1888 at Crabb Island by B. P. and R. L. Miles. Her hull is "chunk built," or made of nine logs, rather than by a plank-and-frame method of construction. Originally rigged for sailing, she was converted to power in 1907, and a new, larger cabin was added aft.

You can cruise on the *Tennison* and see the Governor Johnson Bridge, the Solomons Island and Chesapeake Biological Laboratory, and the U.S. Naval Recreation Center at Point Patience. This is seeing the inner harbor and Patuxent River as you can never see them on land. Captain Rudy Bennett runs the one-hour cruise at 2:00 P.M. Wednesday through Sunday (minimum of ten people required) between May 1 and October 1, or you can charter the boat for your own event. Fares range from $3.50 per adult, $2.50 per child (5 to 12), or $12 per family (regardless of size) to $125 per hour for the charter. Call (410) 326–2042 for additional information.

The Calvert Marine Museum is open daily 10:00 A.M. to 5:00 P.M.

Drum Point Lighthouse

except New Year's, Easter, and Christmas days. A wheelchair is available, but the lighthouse is not handicapped accessible. Admission is $4.00 for adults, $2.00 for children 2 to 5, and $3.00 for seniors 55 and over. You can contact the Calvert Marine Museum at P.O. Box 97, Solomons 20688, or call (410) 326–2042.

Contained within the 327-acre park known as ◆ **Flag Ponds Nature Park** are wooded uplands, ponds, swamps, freshwater marshes, sandy beaches, and part of Chesapeake Bay. Here you can clearly see the difference between the uplands and the wetlands, between the Cliffs of Calvert and Chesapeake Bay. Wildlife abounds, including fox, muskrat, otter, turkey, whitetail deer, and pileated woodpecker. Special facilities include 3 miles of gentle hiking trails, rare plants such as the blue flag iris (from which the park derives its name), pond observation decks, picnic sites, a beach, a fishing pier, and a visitors center with wildlife exhibits. One building remains from what was once a thriving "pound net" fishery that supplied trout, croaker, and herring to the bustling Baltimore markets during the first half of this century. From April 1 through October 1 there is a daily vehicle charge of $4.00 for residents and $6.00 for nonresidents, or a seasonal pass for $15.00 and $20.00, respectively. From November through March the charge is $3.00 for both residents and nonresidents. Flag Ponds is open from 9:00 A.M. to 6:00 P.M. daily and 9:00 A.M. to 8:00 P.M. on weekends during the summer. From Labor Day through Memorial Day the park is open from 9:00 A.M. to 6:00 P.M. and closed during the week.

Herman E. Schieke, Tourism Specialist for Calvert County, invites you to "Discover a place where there are still places to discover." For more information write to Calvert County Department of Economic Development & Tourism, Courthouse, Prince Frederick 20678, or call (800) 331–9771, (410) 535–4583, or (410) 535–6355 (TDD). You can also contact them at their Internet address at http://www.co.cal.md.us.

CHARLES COUNTY

Most of the usual tourist attractions in Charles County are centered in La Plata and Port Tobacco (one of the oldest communities on the East Coast). On the eastern and western "ends" of the county, however, are two interesting views of early Charles County.

On the northeasternmost tip of Charles County is the town of ❖ **Benedict**, named for Benedict Leonard Calvert, the fourth Lord Baltimore. It was a flourishing town at least three times. The first was a period between 1817 and 1937, when steamboats carrying freight and passengers stopped here on their way to and from Baltimore and ports on the Rappahannock and Potomac rivers. The second time was when slot machines were legal in the county and people came to gamble from as far north as New Jersey and New York. The third time was in 1988, when the Governor Thomas Johnson Bridge from Solomons Island to St. Mary's was temporarily closed. Ferries were put in service, but many people detoured to Benedict and used the Patuxent River Bridge. Benedict is also notable as the landing site for 4,500 British troops in August 1814. Local historians say it is the only small town on United States soil that has been invaded by foreign troops, for these were the troops who marched on to the nation's capital. The British troops returned to Benedict with their wounded, and two of their soldiers were buried at Old Fields Chapel cemetery in Hughesville. During the Civil War, Camp Stanton was established here for recruiting and training black infantrymen to serve in the Union Army.

Today this waterside town, the farthest inland port on the Patuxent River, has a post office (Dolores Buick is the postmaster) that is also a paperback lending library, a restaurant or two, and some "boatels" for storing boats. Sue and Maurice Roach own Benedict Pier Restaurant and Marina, and Chappelear's is owned by Francis and Katherine Chappelear (an old Benedict family), who harvest some of the oysters they serve and buy "peeler" crabs for their delectable soft shells. Veer off to the right of Route 231, just before the bridge, if you are looking for dockside atmosphere.

On the northwestern tip is ❖ **Marshall Hall,** which for three-quarters of a century was an amusement park for the young, the young-at-heart, and young lovers from around the Washington, D.C., area. Originally Marshall Hall was a thriving eighteenth-century plantation owned by the William Marshall family. By 1725 Thomas Marshall had built a Georgian-style mansion and outbuildings, including a pier that extended into the Potomac River in a direct line with the entrance road, dividing the plantation into two mirrored halves. It is said that George Washington visited here frequently from his home across the river at Mount Vernon.

Due to financial losses from the Civil War, the Marshall family lost the property in 1866. It passed through a number of owners before the Mount Vernon and Marshall Hall Steamboat Company bought the estate in 1895 to develop it into a Victorian amusement park with gardens, croquet and jousting greens, gazebos, and concession stands.

The amusement park was torn down in the 1920s to be replaced by a more modern park, the one we natives remember. An evening at Marshall Hall started with a boat ride down the Potomac, past Mount Vernon on the right, to Marshall Hall. A few hours of rides and games, and then it was a boat ride back to Washington.

Discussions are held regularly about doing something with this property, but at this time there are only memories of the amusement park and some remnants of the mansion. Three walls stand eerily silhouetted in a morning fog together with a brick outbuilding and the Marshall family cemetery, a fenced burial ground of about twenty-four known graves, half of which date back to the 1700s. The view of Mount Vernon across the river is still there as well. Marshall Hall is open daily and admission is free. To reach Marshall Hall, take Route 210 about 12 miles south of the Capital Beltway to Route 227. Turn right and follow the road about 5 miles to its end. Marshall Hall will be on your right; a large parking lot and boat ramp will be on your left.

On the other (north) side of the Charles County/Prince George's County line is National Colonial Farm, which is open Tuesday through Sunday. Call (410) 283–2113.

In between these two historic spots is ❖**Mount Carmel Monastery,** the first convent for religious women in colonial America, founded on October 15, 1790. It was started by four Carmelite nuns, three of whom—Ann, Ann Theresa, and Susan Mathews—along with the Reverend Charles Neale were natives of Charles County. The group set up temporary quarters at Chandler's Hope, then owned by the Neale family. Father Neale donated 860 acres to the Carmelites to build their monastery. Two of the original convent buildings have been restored and are open to visitors during the summer season. The other buildings are still used as an active convent.

If you are driving in from Route 301 on Mitchell Road, Mt. Carmel Monastery is on the left about ½ mile past Charles County Community College on Mt. Carmel Road. The monastery is open from 8:00 A.M. to 4:00 P.M. Mass is said daily at 7:15 A.M. and on Sunday at 8:00 A.M. Call (410) 934–1654.

Across from the monastery on Mitchell Road, on the Community College property, is ❖**Friendship House,** one of the oldest homes in the county. This four-room, hall-and-parlor–style house was built by William Dent in 1680 on Nanjemoy Creek. In 1968 it was dismantled by the Historical Society of Charles County and moved to its current location. Openings have been left in the structure so visitors can view the seventeenth-century construction techniques.

Friendship is open for tours and a ten- to fifteen-minute slide presentation from noon to 4:00 P.M. on Saturday and Sunday, May through September. Tours by appointment are available at other times. There is a nominal admission charge. Call (410) 934–2251, extension 610, for information on Friendship House from the Southern Maryland Studies Center at Charles County Community College.

In your travels through the county, you may see evidence of tobacco, an important (and maybe the most important) crop in this area for 300 years. It takes 250 man-hours to produce one acre of tobacco (less labor-intensive crops may take as little as four man-hours), and Maryland tobacco is air-dried in a "stick" of tobacco made up of individually harvested leaves. In contrast, Virginia tobacco is flue-cured by heat in three days, and the entire plant is cut at one time. During the three- to six-month drying or curing process, each stick of tobacco will lose more than one-and-a-half gallons of water.

◆ **Tobacco auctions** are held every spring at Hughesville, Waldorf, and La Plata, and visitors are welcome to attend the auctions and tour the warehouses. However, as tobacco is replaced with less labor-intensive crops and as urbanization encroaches into Charles County, fewer farmers are planting tobacco and the auctions have been reduced in number. If you will be here between mid-March and early May, you can get auction schedules and directions by calling the Farmer's Warehouse (410–274–3124), Hughesville Warehouse (410–274–3101), or Edelen Brothers Warehouse (410–934–2601).

◆ **Pope's Creek** is the best place to go for crabs and a view of the Potomac River. The 3-mile drive down Pope's Creek Road is also a little history lesson, for it was along this route that John Wilkes Booth found refuge after assassinating Abraham Lincoln. Two historical markers designate where he stopped along Pope's Creek Road for three days and where he crossed the Potomac into Virginia. (Dr. Samuel A. Mudd's house, where Booth was treated, is farther north in the county on Route 232, south of Route 382. It is open for tours from March to November, with a $2.00 admission charge for adults; call (410) 934–8464 or (410) 743–3837.)

Down at Pope's Creek are the shells of oysters eaten over the centuries, first by Charles County Indians, then by settlers, and today by travelers. These shells cover some thirty acres to a depth of 15 feet in some places. If you prefer eating crabs and oysters to looking at old shells, stop by Robertson's, Captain Billy's, or Pier 3 for some crabs served in a traditional style. The tables are covered with paper and piles of those tasty crabs; a pitcher of beer accompanies the feast. Here you can learn why Maryland is called the Land of Pleasant Living. The old building on your right as you drive to the water is an old Rural Electrification Administration powerhouse with lovely arched windows reminiscent of the Palladian style.

The bridge across the Potomac, 3 miles downriver, is the Governor Harry W. Nice Bridge. It opened in 1940, replacing Laidlow's Ferry, and was the first crossing of the Potomac River south of the nation's capital. The 1938 ground breaking was presided over by President Franklin D. Roosevelt. The bridge is 1⅔ miles long, rises 135 feet above the water, and carries nearly four million vehicles yearly. Passenger cars pay a 75-cent toll in either direction.

For additional tourism information, write to Joanne Roland, Tourism Officer, Charles County, P.O. Box B, La Plata 20646, or call (410) 934–0107.

ST. MARY'S COUNTY

There are some counties in Maryland that are off the beaten path even when you are on their most-traveled roads. St. Mary's is one of them. The county offers many different attractions that draw thousands of people each year, yet it remains primarily historic and underdeveloped. From the Naval Air Test and Evaluation Museum (connected with the Naval Air Station, Patuxent River), to the Old Jail Museum, to Point Lookout State Park with its terrific camping area and beaches, to the crafts at Cecil's Mill and Christmas Country Store, you can spend a good deal of time down here.

Historic St. Mary's City was the first proprietary colony in America and the first capital of Maryland. There are still numerous traces of colonial times, including Sotterley Plantation, an eighteenth-century working plantation overlooking the Patuxent River. At the St. Clements Island Potomac River Museum you can discover the landing site of Maryland's first European settlers. Historic churches abound.

St. Mary's City is actually a small town—just St. Mary's College, a post office, Trinity Episcopal Church, and Historic St. Mary's

City, an outdoor living-history museum. Scant development and modernization has meant that St. Mary's is the only early permanent English settlement that has remained largely undisturbed; thus it is a favorite of archaeologists, who have uncovered millions of artifacts in a relatively short time.

While visiting Historic St. Mary's City, you can see the replica of the square-rigged *Maryland Dove*, one of the two ships that brought the first settlers and supplies from England; the reconstructed State House of 1676; the Godiah Spray Tobacco Plantation; archaeological excavations; Farthing's Ordinary (a seventeenth-century inn exhibit and modern restaurant); the Margaret Brent Memorial Garden; and a visitors center with an archaeology exhibit hall, guided walking tours, and museum gift shop. The exhibits are open from March 24 through the last weekend in November, Wednesday through Sunday 10:00 A.M. to 5:00 P.M. Call (301) 862–0990.

With more miles of shoreline than square miles of land and a college campus full of students, you know this has to be a good party town. One can study only so long. St. Mary's College was St. Mary's Female Seminary, and it is considered one of the best buys in education, with an excellent teacher-student ratio and a small enrollment of about 1,300 students. And the Potomac and Patuxent rivers, the creeks, the streams, and Chesapeake Bay are ideal for biology and marine science studies. But the bay also makes this area ideal for sailing, so it is frequently invaded by sailors seeking a home port. The annual Governor's Cup Regatta is considered one of the ten best sailing parties of the year by national sailors. The water is also perfect for those interested in sailboarding. With St. Mary's mild winters, students can enjoy boating about six months of the school year.

The ◆ **Freedom of Conscience Statue** at the entrance to the college was erected by the counties of Maryland and symbolizes the religious freedom on which the state was founded. In 1649, at the request of town officials from St. Mary's City, a guarantee of freedom of conscience to all Christians (freedom of other religions came later) was enacted by the state legislature.

All is not water, water, everywhere, in St. Mary's County; some of the area is devoted to produce farms. One of the major enticements of the county is the Charlotte Hall Farmers Market with its Amish goods, produce, antiques, and curios. As with most farmer's markets, the earlier you arrive, the better the selection. The market is on Route 5 in Charlotte Hall. Call (301) 884–3966 or 884–3108. I met potter Michael Olson at his ◆ **Toddy Hall Pottery** many years ago when I was researching my first article about St. Mary's County. As I recall, he was tired of the rat race of professional teaching and had "retired" to the quiet life of his relatives from St. Mary's County. One of his objectives had been to re-create the pottery of the early St. Mary's settlers, and his "St. Mary's work" is available. He also produces some Colonial Williamsburg pieces.

I stopped by his studio, loved his work, and bought a flowerpot, although I have been known to kill even plastic greenery. Toddy Hall Pottery thrives today and is still focused on beauty and quality, and you can buy pitchers, cups, bowls, and other ceramics. Olson also is creating sculptures and paintings these days.

The address for Toddy Hall Pottery is P.O. Box 64, Cherryfield Road, Drayden 20630. Take Route 5 south through Leonardtown, turn south on Route 249 at Callaway, then east on Route 244 (the Drayden Road) at Valley Lee, and follow the signs. Call (301) 994–0947 for hours.

The *Captain Tyler* passenger ferryboat runs between Point Lookout State Park and Smith Island, with the 100-minute ride departing at 10:00 A.M. and returning at 4:00 P.M. It operates daily from Memorial Day through Labor Day, other times on Saturday and Sunday, and can carry 150 passengers. The cost is $20 for adults and $10 for children; bicycles are permitted and are included in the fare. For more information call Tyler's Cruises, Rhodes Point 21858 (410–425–2771).

One of the newest attractions in this county that is still making history is the ◆ **Piney Point Lighthouse Museum and Park.** This is where you can see exhibits describing the construction and operation of the lighthouse (which was in use from 1836 through 1964) and the role of the United States Coast Guard. The lighthouse was the first permanent lighthouse built on the Potomac River and is the only remaining accessible lighthouse on its original location in Southern Maryland.

The *Black Panther* is a U-1105 German submarine from World War II days that featured a rubber coating that made it "invisible" to the detection devices of the day. The sub was captured at the end of the war, and after going over it with a fine-tooth comb, the United States Navy sank it off the coast of Piney Point. Now it's Maryland's first **Historic Shipwreck Diving Preserve** and a National Historic Landmark.

There is a six-acre park surrounding the lighthouse and the museum, which are open seven days a week from sunrise to sunset. The museum and gift shop are open weekends from noon to 5:00 P.M. May through October. Call (301) 769–2222 for weekday hours.

For additional tourism information, write to Cindy Woodburn, St. Mary's County Division of Tourism, P.O. Box 653, Leonardtown 20650. Call (800) 327–9023.

Freedom of Conscience Statue

UPPER EASTERN SHORE

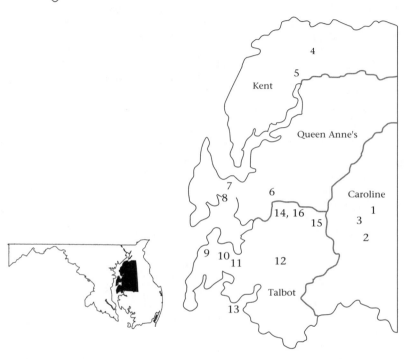

1. Museum of Rural Life
2. Wye Oak Sculpture
3. Ashly Acres
4. Kent Museum
5. Bicycle tours
6. Old Wye Grist Mill
7. Holly's Restaurant
8. Horsehead Wetland Center
9. Museum of Costume
10. St. Mary's Square Museum
11. Inn at Perry Cabin
12. John S. McDaniel House
    Bed and Breakfast
13. Tred Avon Ferry
14. Orrell House and Bakery
15. Tidewater Inn and
    Conference Center
16. Wye Oak State Park

Upper Eastern Shore

On the eastern side of the Chesapeake Bay lies the Eastern Shore, a very distinct and separate entity from the "western shore." People here are dedicated to the ways of the watermen and to the riches the land can bring, although farming here means just about anything that grows (except tobacco). At the eastern end of the William Preston Lane Jr. Memorial Bridge—the Chesapeake Bay Bridge—is Kent Island, where the first European settlement in Maryland was founded in 1631. When the settlers came, they found the Nanticoke and Choptank tribes, which are now immortalized by Indian lore exhibits and two rivers named after the tribes.

History surrounds the bay's little towns and 500 sheltered harbors. The bay is home to boatbuilders, sailors, fishermen (10,000 fishermen earn their livelihood from the bay), and sportsmen. The waterways are often as secluded as in the days when pirates and buccaneers hid in the bays and inlets. Some say there may still be buried treasure stashed in the sand dunes.

Hunters flock here every fall, for this is a major stop for migrating birds on the Atlantic flyway. To conserve and protect those birds that are not so abundant, nearly $2 million have been raised for conservation projects along the flyway.

On the flat-as-a-pancake terrain are farmlands, stately manors, and, once again, small towns. It seems that most of Maryland is filled with small towns. And, fortunately, the towns of the Eastern Shore are always sponsoring festivals celebrating the richness of the land or the sea.

Kent, Queen Anne's, Caroline, and Talbot counties offer many riches. In them I explore a farmer's market, the remains of an oak tree, some eateries, a few bed-and-breakfast places, miniature horses that are not the ponies of Assateague and Chincoteague, bicycle tours to get you exploring the gentle countryside, a very old gristmill, a few museums, and the best biscuits you will ever have.

Caroline County

Caroline County is the only Eastern Shore county not directly on the ocean or the bay, but there are calm waters, such as the

92

Choptank and Tuckahoe Rivers and Marshyhope Creek, state parks for canoeing and fishing, and an active crabbing and fishing industry. The prime interest here is agrarian and the crops are bountiful. Corn, soybeans, cucumbers, tomatoes, peas, beans, sweet corn, cantaloupes, peaches, and melons fill the fields and make a stop at a local produce stand an essential part of anyone's visit.

Across from the Caroline County Courthouse in Denton is the brand new ◆ **Museum of Rural Life.** Even county residents realize that the farming folk who have populated Caroline for the past three centuries may as well have been "consigned to a black hole of obscurity." The county has produced no national leaders, scientists, engineers, patriots, or even notorious rogues. Tombstones are the only proof that people have indeed lived here throughout the history of the United States.

Now, thanks to J. O. K. Walsh, the Denton Jaycees, the County Historical Society, and who knows who else, a determined effort has produced this musuem, a tribute to those anonymous farming families who created Caroline County history. The museum combines one of the original dwellings on Court House Square with new construction. There's a reception area, gallery for rotating exhibits, and an audiovisual room. The museum explores the various aspects and changes in rural life since European settlers arrived here in the 1600s. Hundreds of artifacts, documents, and photographs have been collected. You may even uncover some of the history behind the fireworks-induced conflagration of July 4, 1865. If for some reason you can't find the answer to your Caroline County history question here, talk with Walsh. He's known as the person who "knows more about Caroline history than anyone." Call (410) 479–0274.

In June 1984, in the quiet hours of an early Sunday night, a thirty-five–ton limb from Maryland's state tree crashed to the ground. Being practical, the state decided that some of the limb should be made into souvenirs, such as gavels; but 70,000 pounds of tree would make a lot of gavels.

The Maryland Forest, Park and Wildlife Service sent a two-ton chunk of wood to sculptor Steven Weitzman to create the ◆ **Wye Oak Sculpture.** He carved the wood into a monument in his shop at Seneca Creek State Park in Gaithersburg. On April 3, 1985, his sculpture of two children leaning over a shovel in the

93

act of planting a tree was moved to its permanent home at Martinak State Park near Denton. The children, carved larger than life-size, are standing beneath a white oak tree in this 10-foot-tall statue that measures about 4½ feet from front to back. Also at Martinak is the reconstructed hull of a wrecked bungy, a type of boat used on the bay in the early nineteenth century. The park is open from sunrise to sunset daily, except Christmas week. Martinak State Park is on Deep Shore Road, off Route 404, Denton; call (410) 479–1619.

The historical marker next to the Choptank Electric Cooperative on Route 404 and 328, just west of Denton, marks the modest but historic Neck Meeting House. Built in 1802 by members of the Society of Friends, the meetinghouse is believed to be the oldest house of worship in Caroline County. Most of the funds raised for the aluminum marker came from the recycling of aluminum cans by local residents. The Choptank Electric Cooperative is refurbishing the small building, and if you would like to look inside, stop by the cooperative for the key.

The Slo Horse Inn is located in a quiet country setting on a twelve-acre horse farm between Ridgely and Denton. Owner Cat (Catherine) Sebasco says it was a horse farm featuring some of the slowest thoroughbred race horses ever born. "They were not known for winning," says Cat. So she and husband Jesse kicked the horses out to pasture and converted the stable into four bedrooms, each with private bath, TV, coffeepot, and refrigerator. You can choose king, queen, double, or twin-bedded accommodations, or combine two rooms for a family or two couples.

"It's very casual out here," she says. In fact, when Cat moved to Caroline from Washington, D.C., she felt like she was trying to "tap dance to a waltz." Now she's acclimated to the different pace and loves it.

Rates are $55 for double occupancy, $42 single, and $65 for a family or two couples. Take Holly Road off Route 404 and continue for exactly 1⁹⁄₁₀ miles; look for a large white farmhouse, with a post-and-rail fence, on the right. Call (410) 634–2128.

❖ **Ashly Acres** produced the first miniature horses to participate in an inaugural parade—former president Bush's. This nine-acre farm is owned by Robin Stallings, Karen Kilheffer, and Ashly Wayne Asbury, who breed, raise, and show quality registered miniature horses.

Wye Oak Sculpture

A miniature horse is a true horse, not a pony or a dwarf, and is very gentle. According to Ashly Acres, the ancestor of the modern miniature horse was bred for the royal courts of Europe during the seventeenth century. The horses were often passed from one sovereign to another as diplomatic tokens of goodwill. When the power and wealth of the royalty began to decline, a few horses found their way into the traveling circuses of Europe. Some were used as pit ponies in the coal mines. The selective breeding process was interrupted, and the breed almost became extinct.

The American miniature horse is a scaled-down model of a full-sized horse and can measure no more than 34 inches at the withers. Foals usually weigh between eighteen and twenty-five pounds and stand between 16 and 22 inches at birth. They come in all colors, and although they can be ridden by very small children, they usually are used in harness where they can easily pull a full-sized adult. They function best as lovable exotic pets.

In the early 1900s, a Virginian named Normal Fields imported some miniature horses with a shipment of pit ponies. He was so taken with them that he started a breeding program that continued for thirty-five years. Another Virginian, Smith McCoy, started with ten or twelve horses under 32 inches and built one of the largest miniature horse herds in the United States.

The address for Ashly Acres is R.D. 1, Box 207CC, Denton 21629. Tours for twenty-five people or more are available by appointment; call (410) 479–1159 to ask if you can join one.

For additional tourism information, write to Caroline County Economic Development Commission, P.O. Box 207, Denton 21629, or call (410) 479–2230.

KENT COUNTY

Kent County has the largest proportion of farmland to total acreage of the Upper Eastern Shore counties, yet it is bordered on the north by the Sassafras River, on the south by the Chester River, and on the west by the Chesapeake Bay, so you can understand its multiple focal points. There might be an Old-Fashioned Fourth festival in Rock Hall, an Eastern Shore fish fry, and a Kent County Watermen's Association workboat race and docking course competition, all on the same summer weekend. After the harvest, it is time for snow goose and deer hunting.

For those who prefer architectural history to land and water sports, Chestertown, the county seat of the smallest county in the state, is said to be the tenth-favorite historic place in America because of the large number of restored eighteenth-century homes. When driving through Kent County, it is wonderful to take time to see local sites, such as the picturesque view of waterfront homes at Chestertown; the Eastern Neck National Wildlife Refuge; the Geddes-Piper House, a Philadelphia-style town house; the Kitty Knight House; the 3,000-acre wildlife research and demonstration area known as Remington Farms; the Rock Hall Museum and the water; and Washington College, the tenth-oldest college in this country, which George Washington helped found.

On the second and fourth Saturdays of the month, Harry Rudnick and Sons auction antiques, furniture, glass, china, Oriental rugs, and almost everything else anyone wants to sell. Frank Rudnick, the son of the late Harry Rudnick, says, "We have dealers, local people, and antique-shop owners, and they come from Pennsylvania, Maryland, Delaware, Virginia, D.C.—all over." The auction starts at 9:00 A.M. and continues to about 4:00 or 4:30 P.M. "We sell about eight hundred, nine hundred, a thousand items a day," says Rudnick.

Whenever there is a sale, the lunchroom is open for breakfast and lunch and the menu changes every week. "Some days," adds Rudnick, "the women prepare spaghetti, fried chicken, or turkey, and there's hamburgers, hot dogs, and homemade soup."

Harry Rudnick and Sons is on Main Street, P.O. Box 190, Galena 21635. Call (410) 648–5601.

At the ✛ **Kent Museum** are indoor and outdoor exhibits of farm machinery from the last two centuries. The county gave a group of local farmers one hundred acres, twenty-five acres of which they ran on a volunteer basis to help defray the museum's operating costs. The museum was started about two decades ago, and people from the area and as far away as Pennsylvania have donated equipment to it.

Two early farm tractors mark the entrance, so you cannot miss it. Inside and outside the 40- by 150-foot building are exhibits on equipment used in planting and harvesting corn, wheat, soy, and other grains. You will see threshers, tools from preindustrial days, and modern-day combines and reapers. Other exhibits explain the work done by hand planters, automated corn planters, and tractors (the earliest tractor on display is a 1947 model).

On the first Saturday in August is a threshing dinner. Of course, if you just happen by at other times of the year when they are planting or otherwise tending to the fields, you can watch them at work then, too.

No admission is charged, but contributions are accepted. Kent Museum is open 10:00 A.M. to 4:00 P.M. the first and third Saturday of the month from April through September, and it is located on Route 448 at Turner's Creek Public Landing, near Kennedyville. Call John Clendaniel at (410) 778–3257 or Mrs. William Payne at (410) 348–5721 for additional information.

◆ **Bicycle tours** are popular in Kent County, and the chamber of commerce has prepared a booklet, "The Kent County Bicycle Tour," for your information. Included are nine routes developed by the Baltimore Bicycling Club that range from 11 to 81 miles in length. As an example, the Pomona Warm-Up is "eleven miles of gently winding country roads with great views of the Chester River. A country store located at Pomona is a good eat or drink stop." The Pump House Primer is "eighty-one miles of gently rolling to flat riding through northern Kent County and on to Cecil County's historic Chesapeake and Delaware Canal Pump House Museum at Chesapeake City. Highlights are the Sassafras River, the museum, the C & D Canal, and Cecil County's beautiful horse farms." Note that you must walk your bike across the Sassafras River bridge.

In addition to tourism information, specific directions, and maps, a listing of restaurants, hotels, motels, campgrounds, and bed-and-breakfast establishments is available. Write to Patricia C. Piposzar, Executive Secretary, Kent County Chamber of Commerce, 400 South Cross Street, Chestertown 21620, or call (410) 778–0416.

QUEEN ANNE'S COUNTY

The ◆ **Old Wye Grist Mill** is the oldest business in Queen Anne's County, in operation since 1664, 1671, or 1680, depending on whose reports you read. At least three mills have been located in this area for more than 300 years, giving the town of Wye Mills its name. Among its historic claims is the fact that ground cornmeal from this mill was purchased by Robert Morris, financier of the American Revolution, to be used as provisions for George Washington's army at Valley Forge in 1778.

Preservation Maryland, an organization to preserve the state's history and culture, has had the pleasure of working on this mill, which is particularly fascinating because as new equipment was developed, the old equipment was not hauled away or discarded. Therefore, there is a continuum of equipment to show the progress of milling over the years. The organization has completed work on the hydraulics and done most of the interior restoration and soon will transfer ownership to the Friends of Wye Mill.

During your visit you can try your skill at Maryland's preindustrial crafts, such as weaving, broom making, and hand milling. Also, depending on the season, you can buy cornmeal and a variety of flours—buckwheat, whole wheat, and, sometimes, rye. Josh Fradel, miller, welcomes your visit.

The Wye Mill is open Monday through Friday 10:00 A.M. to 1:00 P.M. and Saturday and Sunday from 10:00 A.M. to 4:00 P.M. in the summer and by appointment at other times. There is no admission charge, but they do ask for a donation. The mill is on Route 50, south of Route 662. The mailing address is P.O. Box 277, Wye Mills 21679, or you can contact the mill at (410) 827–6909 or 685–2886.

Queen Anne's is known for its sprawling countryside and 900 farms, its terrific access to the bay and bay tributaries, and the genteel lifestyle it promotes. Kent Narrows, formerly known for its horrendous weekend beach traffic jams, has become a minor destination of its own, with plenty of historic sites, fine boating, golf, and dining.

Queen Anne's is becoming known for something else, too—factory outlet stores. Chesapeake Village Outlets, at Queenstown, is just east of the Route 301–50 split.

You will notice a number of restaurants in Queen Anne's County, and a few merit some special mention: Hemingway's (Stevensville, 410–643–CRAB) and Annie's Paramount Steak House (Routes 50 and 30 at Mears Point, 410–827–7605). Both have excellent seafood and docking facilities.

The meeting place of the Eastern Shore since 1955, however, has been ❖ **Holly's Restaurant,** noted for having the best milkshakes in the state. The tables are wooden and devoid of such frills as tablecloths, the waitresses are friendly, and the servings are enormous. You will find Holly's off Route 50 in Grasonville. Call (410) 827–8711.

Birdlife photographers and observers will enjoy the new ✦ **Horsehead Wetland Center** and the adjacent captive wildfowl collection in Grasonville. Surrounded by more than 300 acres of natural beauty, the center has a fascinating and colorful flock of wildfowl, including ducks, geese, and swans, and nearby are deer, red foxes, river otters, and bald eagles. Special screening allows you to quietly enter blinds so you can observe wildlife without disturbing it. The observation tower offers a panoramic view of Chesapeake Bay and its wetlands.

The Wildfowl Trust of North America, founded in 1979, is responsible for the center, and you can be sure of programs, guided walks, workshops, a wetland festival, and lectures promoting stewardship of our dwindling wetland resources. A gift shop and a shaded picnic area are also on-site.

Horsehead Wetland Center is ½ mile from Route 18, off Perry Corner Road. Admission is $3.00 for adults, $2.00 for senior citizens, and $1.00 for children. Dogs are not permitted. The center is open 9:00 A.M. to 5:00 P.M. Wednesday through Sunday. It is closed July 4, Thanksgiving, Christmas, and New Year's Day. For more information write to Benedict J. Hren, Executive Director, The Wildfowl Trust of North America, P.O. Box 519, Grasonville 21638, or call (410) 827–6694.

For years the yellow and blue can of Old Bay Seasoning has been the only one to put on the table with that pile of steaming crabs. Then in the mid-1960s, cousins Joe Bernard and Mike Rossbach decided to can some Wye River Crab Soup, and that led to Wye River crab spices, and Wye River potato chips and tortilla chips—these two young men have started an entire industry. Most of the ingredients for the white or red crab soup (claw meat, potatoes, tomatoes, lima beans, carrots, and green beans) are grown right here in Maryland. There is no factory to tour, for the soup is made in New Jersey and the chips are made in Ohio, but you can stop by the headquarters and buy from their full line of products.

Wye River Products is in Queenstown at Green Spring Road, Route 50. Call (410) 643–2666.

For more tourism information, write to Queen Anne's County

Office of Tourism, 3100 Main Street, Grasonville 21638. Call (410) 827–4810.

TALBOT COUNTY

Tourists coming through this area—about 100,000 each year going to St. Michaels—stop to see the Chesapeake Bay Maritime Museum, the Customs House, the Robert Morris Inn, and Tilghman Island (with a meal at Harrison's Chesapeake House).

The Chesapeake Bay Maritime Museum receives by far the most tourists, and well it should. But there are two small, privately owned museums that may also be worth your time.

Millie Curtis's ◆**Museum of Costume** in St. Michaels contains some unique displays. On exhibit are gowns worn by former presidents' wives, pantaloons worn by Mrs. Abraham Lincoln, and a vest worn by Clark Gable in *Gone With the Wind*. Rooms are filled with ornate nineteenth- and early twentieth-century gowns. Curtis has been accumulating her collection since 1940. She has been known to greet guests wearing one of her costumes.

Also of interest is the setting, representing life as it was for the wealthy and the not-so-wealthy. Ms. Curtis herself is a wealth of information and a fascinating conversationalist, so you might want to plan a little extra time to enjoy your trip to the past.

The white frame house was erected by shipbuilder and sea captain Lewis Tarr in 1843. It is restored so you can see the original pine floors, the board-and-batten doors, and other aspects of the architecture.

The Museum of Costume is open weekends 11:00 A.M. to 4:00 P.M., April through November. The suggested donation is $2.00. Children under 10 are admitted free. The address is 400 St. Mary's Square, St. Michaels 21663. Call (410) 745–5154.

◆**St. Mary's Square Museum** exhibits items of significance to the local history and culture, not just of St. Michaels, but of the land between Tilghman and Royal Oak, called the Bay 100— that portion of land that could be defended by one hundred armed men. Two buildings are used for this museum, one of them dating from 1820 and one from 1860, the latter referred to as the "Teetotum" building because it looks like the shape of a child's four-sided top of that name.

In the 1820 building are artifacts from 1800 to 1850; in the

101

kitchen area are items from 1850 to 1900; and in the Teetotum room are articles from colonial days to about 1950. Curator Horace Wilson says most of these buildings were moved from other sites in the area. This museum was opened in 1964 by a group of local citizens, and although it sits on the original St. Mary's Square and is on city property, the museum is entirely self-supported. A group of twenty board members runs the operation. The museum is open from May through October on Saturday, Sunday, and on holidays from 10:00 A.M. to 4:00 P.M. and by appointment. There is no admission charge, but donations are accepted. For additional information call (410) 745–9561.

Laura Ashley fans rejoice. Sir Bernard Ashley (who with his late wife, Laura, founded the clothing and furnishings empire) has added even more rooms to his ❖ **Inn at Perry Cabin** in St. Michaels. You now have a choice of forty-one individually and sumptuously decorated rooms and suites that include many Laura Ashley design touches. There's also an indoor pool and exercise room. The food is superb, the wine cellar extraordinary, and the setting as picture-perfect for a wedding as anyone could wish. Bring your boat and dock at the inn's slips.

Pick up one of the inn's bicycles to explore the countryside (nice and flat, and very pastoral) or just come to relax.

From April through December, rates range from $195 to $575, including a full breakfast and afternoon tea. From January through March, the rates have been known to drop. Also, frequent visitors have been treated to upgrades when available, without even asking. This is hospitality in a fine tradition.

Inn at Perry Cabin is at 308 Watkins Lane, St. Michaels 21663. The phone number is (410) 745–5178.

A stop in St. Michaels isn't complete until you've stopped by **Flamingo Flats,** which sells hundreds and hundreds of hot pepper sauces. Owner Bob Deppe notes that the hot pepper sauce craze is about a $350 million business and he's eager to be part of it. Among the sauces you'll find are Chile Today Hot Tamale, Gator Hammock Gator Sauce, Jump Up and Kiss Me, Lottie's Bajan Cajan, Matouk's Hot Calypso, Ring of Fire, and Rothschild's Fiery Raspberry Salsa. If you have an asbestos tongue, step up to the tasting bar and go to town.

The shop specialty is its own Cannonball sauce. Cannonball is a combination of carrots, onions, lime juice, tomato, vinegar, and habanera peppers. It's a sauce more for tasting than for destroying your intestinal lining.

Flamingo Flats is located at 406 Talbot Street, St. Michaels 21663. Call (410) 745–2053 or (800) HOT–8841.

Bed-and-breakfast establishments seem to belong in large Victorian homes, and the ◆ **John S. McDaniel House Bed and Breakfast,** operated by Dawn Rehbein, fits that description to a T. Built about 1890, the house has a high octagonal tower (a great sitting room), a hip-roof with dormers, and a porch that runs across the front and part of the south side of the house. Each of the eight guest rooms is spacious and bright and equipped with air-conditioning and a ceiling fan. Fortunately, the house is located within walking distance of historic Easton. Room rates run from $75 to $110 and include a continental breakfast served between 8:00 and 10:00 A.M.

The John S. McDaniel House Bed and Breakfast is located at 14 North Aurora Street, Easton 21601. Call (410) 822–3704 for information and reservations.

Another wonderful lodging place in Easton is the ◆ **Tidewater Inn and Conference Center.** The Tidewater looks ages old and is filled with eighteenth-century furnishings, but it actually was built in 1949 and enlarged in 1953. It's a question of whether the service, the restaurant, or the ambience wins the contest for "best" feature of this hotel.

The service has been impeccable every time I've stopped by. The menu changes with the seasons, and the kitchen staff will work to prepare what you want the way you want it. A grand time to be here is during duck season, when hunters stay; enjoy a 4:30 A.M. hunt breakfast on a chilly autumn moring, then leave before dawn to sit out in the blinds and await your prey. The hotel will arrange guide services and kennel your dogs. And although the property is relatively new, you wouldn't be blamed if you felt the company of past cotillions, proms, and weddings.

Another marvelous feature of the Tidewater is its convenience to shopping, the restored 1921 Avalon Theater, and the Academy of Arts.

All in all, the Tidewater Inn is a superb place to stay as a base for your Eastern Shore sightseeing. It's located at 101 East Dover Street, Easton 21601; call (410) 822–1300.

One of the ten remaining ferries in service in Maryland is the

◆ **Tred Avon Ferry,** which crosses Tred Avon River and connects Oxford to Bellevue. It has been operating since 1683 and is said to be the oldest "free-running" (not cable-connected), privately owned ferry in the country. It operates all year from March 1 through mid-December. The ferry schedule starts at 7:00 A.M. on weekday mornings and 9:00 A.M. on weekends, and runs until sunset, except during June, July, and August, when it runs until 9:00 P.M. It costs $4.50 for car and driver one way and $7.00 round-trip plus 50 cents per passenger each way. Bicycles are $1.50 each way and foot passengers are $1.00 each.

This is a particularly photogenic ferry crossing at sunset, when the boats are all at their Oxford harbor moorings with their masts standing out against the skyline. Next to the Oxford landing is the custom house, a replica of the original built in pre-Revolutionary War days when Oxford was an official port of entry.

To reach the Tred Avon Ferry from Easton, take Route 33 and Route 333; from Bellevue take Route 33 and Route 329 to Royal Oak and follow the signs. Call (410) 745–9023 for further information.

Almost as good as a platter of crabs are the biscuits from ◆ **Orrell House and Bakery.** Hundreds of dozens of these heavy biscuits, which started as a source of pin money for Mrs. Orrell about fifty years ago, go out to local stores and shops around the country. The recipe, which combines flour, water, salt, lard, sugar, and baking powder, originated in Southern Maryland and the Eastern Shore during plantation days. It produces a biscuit that is soft and doughy on the inside and hard on the outside. There are some who say these biscuits are not any good until they feel like hockey pucks, and many swear by them as teething biscuits. Believe me, just because they feel hard does not mean they have gone stale. A special pick is used to prick the tops of the biscuits (in an O and cross design) so they will not blister and burn.

The bakery is open on Wednesday from 7:00 A.M. to 2:00 P.M., Thursday from 2:00 to 11:00 P.M., and Friday from 7:00 A.M. to noon. The address is Orrell House and Bakery, P.O. Box 7, Wye Mills 21679. Turn right at the stoplight at Chesapeake College and drive to the famous Wye Oak Tree. Orrell House is between the oak and Wye parish. Call (410) 822–2065.

◆ **Wye Oak State Park** is considered a "big little" place: The park in total size is only twenty-nine acres, but it contains the 450-year-old Maryland state tree, the Wye Oak. This tree measures a huge 37 feet in circumference and is considered to be the largest and finest of its species in the United States. The state bought the tree and one acre around it in 1939—the first time any state ever purchased one tree just to preserve it. Over time, more land was added to make this a state park. It was the first state park to be fully accessible to the handicapped, perhaps because it's so small that accessibility was easy to create. Wye Oak State Park is south of Wye Mills on Route 662.

You have heard that big oaks come from little acorns, and, of course, the converse is true—little acorns come from big oaks. The Maryland Forest, Park and Wildlife Service gathers the acorns, plants them, and lets them grow for a couple of years until they are established seedlings. You can purchase a Wye Oak seedling from the state for about $6.00 (plus tax if you live in Maryland). They are shipped in March in time for spring planting. They cannot be shipped to Arizona, California, Florida, Louisiana, or Oregon due to quarantine restrictions.

These are the cutest little trees, no bigger in diameter than your little finger, but they produce mature-size leaves, about six or seven of them the first year. They do not grow as rapidly as, say, a maple tree, but they are of substantial size within a decade. And, who knows, 400 years from now there may be a champion tree in your yard.

To order Wye Oak seedlings, write to the Nursery Manager, Buckingham Forest Tree Nursery, Harmans 21077. You must give a full street address; a post office box number is inadequate for delivery.

For more tourism information write to Stephanie Price, Talbot County Chamber of Commerce, P.O. Box 1366, 805 Goldsborough Road, Easton 21601, or call (410) 822–4606.

SOUTHERN EASTERN SHORE

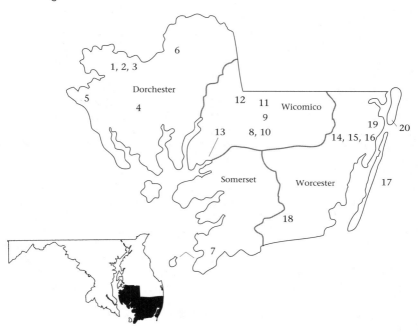

1. Dorchester County Public Library
2. Dorchester Arts Center
3. Wild Goose Amber Beer
4. Blackwater National Wildlife Refuge
5. Taylor's Island General Store
6. East New Market
7. Captain's Galley Restaurant
8. Country House
9. Salisbury Pewter
10. Ward Museum of Wildfowl Art
11. High Ball
12. Mason-Dixon line
13. Ferryboats
14. Berlin walking tour
15. Taylor House Museum
16. Atlantic Hotel
17. Assateague Island National Seashore
18. Pocomoke City Post Office
19. Airplane advertising
20. Phillips Crab House

Southern Eastern Shore

We have reached the easternmost portion of Maryland, the southern part of the DelMarVa Peninsula (*DEL*aware, *MAR*yland, and *Virgini*A), where James Michener conducted the research for his popular novel *Chesapeake*. This is where you see as well as hear about those unfamiliar boats, the skipjack, the bugeye, and the bungy.

You will also see "June bugs," the thousands of kids who invade the ocean beaches and boardwalks every summer to work at jobs and on tanning.

Explore and enjoy the dissimilarities you will find within a few short miles. Stop by a library to see a mural painted by an artist who is so popular these days that the library could not afford another mural like it. Find budding artists at the Dorchester Arts Center. Try a new beer, search for bald eagles and great blue herons, mingle with area residents at the general store, and see centuries-old homes that have not needed restoration because they have been so well maintained over the years.

Ride the ferryboats, eat at some of the best seafood restaurants in the country, examine the fine local examples of duck-decoy carving, and take a peek at some of the prettiest passenger boats and ferryboats being built these days. Take time to locate the Mason-Dixon line; it surprises most people that the line not only separates Pennsylvania and Maryland, but it also delineates the Delaware-Maryland border.

Last but not least, get some sand between your toes and contemplate the treasures of America in Miniature.

Dorchester County

By mid-to-late 1997, when you come over the Cambridge bridge, you'll see something that looks like a large skipjack. It's the new Cultural and Visitors Center at **Sailwinds Park,** and the mistake is understandable because the center will lie amidst two spectacular fiberglass sails. Sailwinds is part of the economic revitalization of Cambridge and Dorchester County; it includes a meeting place, classrooms, a festival area, and more. Already such diverse events as crafts shows, flower shows, pageants, a seafood festival, a Native American powwow, and a beer festival have been held there.

Years before I thought about writing this book, I stopped at the ❖ **Dorchester County Public Library** and admired a wonderful mural of Eastern Shore scenes being painted by the recently deceased Chesapeake Bay artist John Moll. That creation has stayed in my mental and metal filing drawers all these years.

Moll became familiar to James Michener when the author was researching *Chesapeake*, and they collaborated on a subsequent book because Michener thought the Oxford resident "not only captured the flavor of my subject but had earned the enthusiasm of those who love the Chesapeake."

Moll's lithographs are known for their faithful characterization of the skipjacks and bay lighthouses he loved. His Christmas cards with Oxford and Annapolis scenes or Baycraft portraits are still popular, and John Moll oils hang in the permanent collection of the Eastern Academy of Arts and in the historic Robert Morris Inn in Oxford.

This gives you an idea how popular the artist is whose work is on the Dorchester County Public Library walls. The address of the library is 303 Gay Street, Cambridge 21613 (410–228–7331).

The ❖ **Dorchester Arts Center** was founded in 1970 and has between 400 and 500 members (mostly from the Cambridge area) including potters, photographers, quilters, stained-glass artists, and basket makers. In addition to regular classes in these and other crafts, the center has two galleries where local work is exhibited and sold. Each month a new exhibit opens with a reception.

During the year, the center sponsors a variety of music, dance, and educational programs, a number of which are free to the public. Each September the sidewalks along historic, brick High Street, with its beautiful period homes, are festooned with the best work of 125 or more of Dorchester County artists. The center is located at 120 High Street, Cambridge 21613; call (410) 228–7782 for more information.

From the visual arts we move to the art of brewing, which brings us to the new Cambridge microbrewery. The first batch of ❖ **Wild Goose Amber Beer,** billed as "The Only Beer for Crabs," was produced in early November 1989. According to brewmaster Alan Pugsley, Wild Goose tastes like a pale English ale. "Chesapeake's Own" microbrewery license allows the brewers to have a bar or restaurant for on-site ales; however, at this time they are distributing the beer only off-site. Tours of the brewery are available through the old Phillips Packing House, which was, during World War II, the second-largest soup-packing house in the country (Campbell's was the first). The tour lasts about an hour, and naturally it includes a wee taste. Individuals can tour for free; groups cost about $2.50 per person. Wild Goose Amber Beer microbrewery is at 20 Washington Street, Cambridge 21613. Call (410) 221–1121.

Another interesting tour is through the **Brooks Barrel Company,** one of the last remaining slack cooperages now operating in America, and the only one in Maryland. Paul Brooks founded the company in 1950, but it wasn't until the mid-1960s that current manager Kenneth Knox erected an outdoor sign announcing the company's existence. Some of the equipment goes back to the turn of the century, for the procedures haven't changed much. After touring the plant, you'll realize what's involved every time you look at a candy barrel, view the miniseries made from Alex Haley's book, *Queen,* or watch Robert Redford's movie *A River Runs Through It.* Only yellow pine trees from DelMarVa are used; they are crafted into planters, kegs, and barrels. Tours (which can be very noisy) are available by appointment.

Brooks Barrel Company, Inc., is at 5228 Bucktown Road, Cambridge 21613-1056. Call (800) 398–BROOKS.

While you're in the Cambridge area, you might want to stop a minute or two at the **Annie Oakley House,** designed and built in 1912 by Wild West sharpshooter Annie Oakley when she and her husband Frank Butler retired to Cambridge. The bungalow is typical of the period, except for a few features characteristic of the Butlers' unique lifestyle. Annie Oakley House is at 28 Bellevue Avenue on Hambrooks Bay, Cambridge.

Another place of interest is the **birthplace of Harriet Tubman,** the "Moses of her people" because of her work in the Underground Railroad that helped free more than 300 slaves. A slave herself, Tubman ran away only to return to DelMarVa nineteen times to free others. During the Civil War she served in the Union army as a nurse, scout, and spy. The Harriet Tubman birthplace is on Green Briar Road. Call (410) 288–0401.

South of Cambridge is the ◆ **Blackwater National Wildlife**

Refuge. I have spent many hours here trying to photograph the great blue heron. The refuge is a marvelous sanctuary of more than 21,000 acres. The refuge boasts the largest nesting population of bald eagles in the East, after Florida. There is a $3.00 charge per car and a $1.00 charge per person on foot or bicycle.

Besides the bald eagle and the great blue heron, you will see black ducks, the endangered DelMarVa fox squirrel, and countless other animals and birds. Do stop by in November and December when the Canada geese fly overhead. Bring your insect repellent in July and August.

Drive south on Route 16 to Route 335 in Church Creek, to Key Wallace Drive and the signs for the refuge. Blackwater National Wildlife Refuge is open Monday through Friday from 8:00 A.M. to 4:00 P.M. and on weekends from 9:00 A.M. to 5:00 P.M., Labor Day through Memorial Day. Call (410) 228–2677 for further information.

The food is good where the locals gather, and one of these gathering places is on Taylor's Island at ◆ **Taylor's Island General Store,** just across Slaughter Creek Bridge, southwest of Cambridge. The best sandwiches and soups in the area are served here, and you will not go wrong with Erlyne Twining's crab soup, oyster chowder, chili, or lima bean soup; meat-based soups sell for $2.00 and non-meat soups sell for $1.50. The crab cakes contain a quarter-pound of crab meat each and go for $3.00. Quite a bargain. Erlyne, her husband, Perry, and their son Terry also sell ice, beer, soda, gas, and groceries and have an interesting display of "old-time stuff" from former general stores.

You will find signs that spell it Taylors Island—usually state signs—and people who spell it Taylor's—usually the locals, because they say the land originally was called Taylor's Folly after the Mr. Taylor who bought the land. I side with the locals on this one. Taylor's Island General Store is on Route 16, Taylor's Island (410–397–3733).

A number of towns in Maryland are architecturally historic, and the buildings have not needed much outside restoration. ◆ **East New Market,** originally Crossroads, is one of those towns. At each of the four entrances to the town stands a church. On Route 16 South, it is Trinity United Methodist; Route 16 North, St. Stephen's Episcopal; Route 14 West, First Baptist; and Route 14 East, Salem German Evangelical and Reformed Church. These churches reflect the diverse denominations represented in this area. Indians dwelled here; the first European mention of the region was in a grant to Henry Sewell dated 1659 in London, England. The first white settler is believed to have been a Quaker, John Edmondson, who came from Virginia in the 1660s to seek religious freedom. Edmondson was followed by the O'Sullivane family, and this historic district contains almost all of their early residences. These homes are the core of the town's colonial architecture, but among the almost seventy-five buildings are a number from the eighteenth, nineteenth, and twentieth centuries. Many of the brick walks laid in 1884 still exist.

The East New Market Heritage Foundation sponsors an annual Candlelight Tour in late December, with admission set at $7.00 for adults and $6.00 for foundation members and seniors. Children twelve years and under, accompanied by an adult, are free.

The East New Market Heritage Foundation is at P.O. Box 112, East New Market 21631. Call (410) 943–8713.

For additional tourism information, write to Winifred J. Roche, Director, Dorchester County Tourism, 203 Sunburst Highway, Cambridge 21613, or call (410) 228–1000 or (800) 522–TOUR. Dorchester County is also on the Internet and can be reached at http://www.bluecrab.org/es.html or via e-mail at dtourism@skipjack.bluecrab.org.

SOMERSET COUNTY

Every endeavor from the sublime to the ridiculous is represented at two Somerset County museums, and both museums are well documented in most state tourism brochures. Depending on your available time, you will want to stop by the Eastern Shore Early Americana Museum at Route 667 and Old Westover Road, in Hudsons Corner. Pack rats and Americana lovers have Lawrence W. Burgess to thank for being a certifiable scavenger. This museum, housed in a converted poultry house, is a monument to the art of accumulation. It contains a little bit of everything, from political buttons to oyster-tonging forks. For hours and information call (410) 623–8324. On the other hand, there is the Governor J. Millard Tawes Historical Museum in Crisfield, with its exhibits pertaining to the late governor, the history and development of the Crisfield seafood industry, local art and folklore, and the life of the area from Indian times to the present. Call (410) 968–2501 for further information. These two museums may contain items about the same time, place, and people, but they sure do come out different.

With a little time, you also might want to stop by the **Teackle Mansion** (used as an Underground Railroad stop by Harriet Tubman) on Sunday afternoon or visit the hundred-room EconoLodge in Princess Anne, which is the first fully operational franchised hotel operated and managed by student interns; they participate in the Hotel and Restaurant Management program at University of Maryland Eastern Shore.

You might want to try some seafood, for this is the self-proclaimed "Seafood Capital of the World," or take a ferry out to Smith Island. For both of these pleasures, you could not come to a more perfect place.

As you drive down to the end of Main Street to watch the boating activity, stop for a meal at the ◆ **Captain's Galley Restaurant.** They are not immodest when they claim to be the "home of the world's best crab cake." The crabs are caught and picked fresh daily from the Chesapeake waters, and then the meat is lightly seasoned with herbs and spices. For a real treat, try the 100 percent backfin crabmeat, fried or broiled. Owner Rich Tonelli's soft-shell–crab sandwich is no slouch either, and during cold-weather days, there is nothing better than one of their apple dumplings to warm up the insides. The local artwork is also a special treat.

Captain's Galley is at the end of Main Street, well within sight of the relatively new pavilion at the end of the city wharf. It overlooks beautiful Tangier Sound. As you dine on delectable seafood, you can watch the watermen of the Chesapeake bring in the bounty of its waters. Call (410) 968–1636 for information or reservations.

Ferries have been leaving Crisfield to the outlying Smith (the only inhabited island accessible exclusively by boat in Maryland) and Tangier islands for years. One of the most enduring is the *Captain Tyler II,* which travels to Smith Island daily from Memorial Day to September 30. This 65-foot, riverboat-style paddlewheeler was built in New York during World War II and was used as a cargo vessel for the military. The departure time for the one-hour-and-ten-minute crossing is 12:30 P.M., and the boat leaves Smith

Island at 5:30 P.M. It takes up to 150 passengers, and bicycles are permitted. The fare is $18.00 for adults and $9.00 for children 6 to 12 and includes free bus transportation to Rhodes Point. Contact Tyler's Cruises, Rhodes Point 21858 (410–425–2771).

The *Captain Evans* ferry operates between Smith Island and Reedville, Virginia, between May and mid-October, departing Reedville at 10:00 A.M. and 4:00 P.M. The 150-passenger boat costs $16.00 per adult, $8.00 for children, and $2.00 per bike.

One other ferry, the *Captain Tyler,* runs between Point Lookout State Park and Smith Island (see St. Mary's County).

Two of Maryland's ten ferries—the Whitehaven and Upper ferries—operate between Somerset and Wicomico counties. Check the Wicomico County section for additional details.

For further tourism information, write to Sandie Marriner, Director, Somerset County Tourism, P.O. Box 243, Princess Anne 21853. Call (410) 651–2968 or (800) 521–9189 (nationwide).

WICOMICO COUNTY

For a long time Salisbury was known as the last great gasp going east (or the first coming west) on the way to the beach at Ocean City. Now, it's a wonderful community in its own right, and you could spend your vacation here and avoid the hot, sweaty, shoulder-to-shoulder, sand- and sunblock-covered visitors catching the rays on the shore.

The ◆ **Country House** in Salisbury is the largest country store in the East and delights all the senses with sounds of soothing music, the smell of potpourri and candles, and the feel of quality merchandise. You'll discover every colonial home furnishing you could wish to find as well as beautiful decorative accessories and old-time candy. Looking for that perfect something for your kitchen, bedroom, or bathroom? It should be here. You can select from an amazing array of curtains, lighting fixtures, pottery, collectibles, furniture, shelving, rugs, baskets, and dried flowers. There are also some Victorian-style items, and the Christmas section is open year-round.

Owners Mike and Norma Delano handpick every item in the store, and they love to stop and talk with their customers. The shop is open Monday through Saturday 10:00 A.M. to 5:30 P.M.;

on Friday night it's open until 8:00 P.M. From Thanksgiving to Christmas the store stays open until 8:00 P.M. Monday through Friday. You'll find the Country House at 805 East Main Street. Call (410) 749–1959.

◆ **Salisbury Pewter,** formed only in 1980, is a company of dedicated workers who believe that although modern technology can be helpful, the most important part of their business is to maintain the heritage of their craft. Many of their methods have been handed down for centuries, and each piece of pewter they create is meticulously handcrafted and contains no lead. They offer a customizing service, and there is one wall with letters of appreciation from elected high officials for a series of pewter pieces created for an appreciation award.

On weekdays you can see the crafters working pewter from raw product to a finished piece of art. Salisbury Pewter is on Highway 13 North. The mailing address is P.O. Box 2475, Salisbury 21801; call (410) 546–1188 or (800) 824–4700 (out of state).

If you hate a zoo that rambles forever and ever and tries to be encyclopedic in its collection, you'll love the smallness and intimacy of Salisbury Zoological Park. The **Salisbury Zoo** was founded by the city to advance animal conservation and environmental awareness. There are about 400 mammals, birds, and reptiles native to the Americas, with major exhibits of spectacled bears, monkeys, jaguars, bison, bald eagles, and a wonderful waterfowl collection. The snug twelve-acre facility embraces a branch of the Wicomico River and has plenty of shade trees, exotic plants, and wildlife, making for a cool, peaceful setting for family outings. No gift or food concessions are in the zoo, but there are plenty nearby, and picnic tables and toilet facilities are inside the park. Admission and parking are free. Pets, however, are not permitted.

The zoo is open daily from Memorial Day to Labor Day from 8:30 A.M. to 7:30 P.M. and until 4:30 P.M. the rest of the year. Group guided tours are available by appointment; call (410) 742–2640. For general information call (410) 548–3188.

Of major note is the ◆ **Ward Museum of Wildfowl Art,** which houses what is perhaps the largest collection of decorative bird carvings in the world, including many antique decoys. The museum is named for internationally renowned waterfowl carvers and painters Lem and Steve Ward of Crisfield, Maryland. During their lifetimes, they produced more than 25,000 decoys and decorative birds, which the men called "counterfeits." Their workshop has been re-created, and on display are more than one hundred fine examples of their old classic hunting decoys as well as their decoratives. Lem did most of the painting, while Steve did most of the carving. Steve died in 1976, and Lem died in 1984 at the age of eighty-eight.

The museum has changing exhibits featuring oils of wild animals or the art of the Northwest Indians. You can experience the story of this Native American art form, decoy carving, from its beginning to the present. And if you don't want to venture into the wetlands yourself with the bugs and the mud, in the museum you can experience the sights and sounds of the wetland habitat of native American wildfowl.

Even the setting is close to spectacular. The waterfront setting overlooks a bird sanctuary where ducks, geese, heron, osprey, and songbirds flock, as though to perform for you.

An on-site gift shop has a wide selection of wildfowl-related items. Hours are Monday through Saturday from 10:00 A.M. to 5:00 P.M. and Sunday from noon to 5:00 P.M. Guided group tours are available. Admission is $4.00 for adults, $3.00 for seniors, and $2.00 for children (K–12); members and preschoolers are free. For further information contact the Ward Foundation at (410) 742–4988.

The Ward Foundation was established to save the art form of decoy carving, which has grown from the carving of working decoys designed to catch birds to the decorative carving of collector's items. The foundation's annual summer seminars at 909 South Schumaker Drive, Salisbury 21801, offer hands-on instruction by some of the most talented artists and teachers in the field, such as Ernie Muehlmatt, Pat Godin, Bill Koelpin, Bob Guge, Larry Bath, and Jim Sprankle. Intensive, weeklong sessions cover such topics as anatomy and research, shaping, texturing, burning, priming and painting, and various brush techniques. Room and board are provided on campus. For information about the seminars, contact the Ward Foundation at the phone number given above.

If you have ever heard the railroad expression about "high balling it down the road" and wondered what it meant, take a visit to Delmar to see the ◆ **High Ball.** (Delmar lies in both

116

Delaware and Maryland; State Street straddles the border. There was a time when the two halves—two mayors, two town councils, two school systems—fought over municipal functions, but things have been patched up for some time.) Along the tracks near State Street you will see a large white ball, which was raised on high to signify that the line was clear, giving rise to the term "high balling." A small museum is housed in the caboose next to the tracks, and it is open by appointment. Call George Truitt at (302) 846-2654.

Driving along the flat stretch of Route 54 west of Delmar near Mardela Springs, you will parallel the southern end of the north-south section of the ◆ **Mason-Dixon line.** One could even say this is the cornerstone of the Mason-Dixon line. A double crownstone was installed in 1768 by Charles Mason and Jeremiah Dixon to settle the boundary disputes between the Penn and Calvert families, whose coats of arms it bears. There is a small parking lot and a brick and wrought-iron pavilion protecting the stones.

Called the Middle Point monument because it marks the middle of the DelMarVa Peninsula, the crownstone also is a triangulation point of the National Geodetic Survey. The stone was broken off at ground level by vandals in 1983, and another stone originally set by colonial surveyors in 1760 was defaced by removal of the Calvert coat of arms. The Maryland Department of Natural Resources and Delaware's State Boundary Commission jointly replaced the monument on October 24, 1985. Protective grillwork to completely enclose the pavilion was also replaced. The previous grillwork had been erected by the Daughters of the American Revolution.

Skipjacks can be seen in the watermen's villages of Deal Island, Chance, and Wenona. Over Labor Day weekend this last fleet of working sailboats races in the Tangier Sound off Deal Island in the annual Skipjack Races.

Two ◆ **ferryboats** continue service, survivors of the many that once linked water-isolated communities on the Wicomico River, between Wicomico and Somerset counties. Both are small, both are free, and both operate all year, weather conditions and tides permitting.

The Upper Ferry crosses between Allen and Route 349 and takes about three minutes. It is run year-round during daylight hours with on-demand service, except on Sunday and major holidays. The Upper Ferry is an outboard-motor–propelled cable ferryboat with no name. A ferry has been running here since at least 1897; the current one has a capacity of two cars plus six passengers, with a maximum vehicle size of five tons gross weight. Bicycles are permitted.

The Whitehaven–Mt. Vernon Cable Ferry, called the *Whitehaven Ferry*, is 6 miles downriver from the Upper Ferry and connects Whitehaven to Widgeon; it has been operating since 1690. The modern ferryboat, the *Som-Wico*, takes about five minutes for a crossing and can hold three cars plus ten passengers. Bikes are permitted. Whitehaven is the oldest incorporated town on the river and once was a vital deepwater port and shipbuilding area.

Both ferries are run by the Wicomico County Road Department. Call (410) 548–4872 for more information.

Contact Lewis R. Carman, Tourism Director, at the Convention and Visitor Bureau, Post Office Box 2333, Salisbury 21802-2333, for further details on tourism, or you can call (410) 548–4914 or (800) 332–8687.

WORCESTER COUNTY

The town of Berlin in Worcester (pronounced like "rooster") County has no connection to the city in Germany; instead, it is a corruption of Burley Inn, the name of the site on which it was constructed.

A guided map for a ❖ **Berlin walking tour** includes a town park and monument dedicated to Commodore Stephen Decatur, a native of Berlin. The oldest homes were built during the Federal period, later homes adopted the Victorian style, and twentieth-century homes are typified by the "bungalow." The walking tour brochure can be picked up at local Berlin businesses.

A typical Federal-style post-and-beam house is the ❖ **Taylor House Museum.** It was built about 1825 and now is used as the town museum. The gable-front house features a Palladian window with Victorian glass, restored wood graining, and a magnificent front doorway with butterfly modillions, sunbursts, and fluted, engaged columns. The house was supposed to be destroyed and replaced by a new post office and parking lot, but it was saved in 1981 by the Berlin Heritage Foundation. With

Skipjack

$100,000 in private donations from the community, the house was restored from its dilapidated condition.

Although Robert J. Henry, who was instrumental in bringing the railroad to Berlin, lived in the house, the most famous occupant was Calvin B. Taylor, the founder of the Calvin B. Taylor Banking Company, which is still in existence. Much of the house and appointments are original to the times that various occupants lived in the house, including C. B. Taylor's bank desk with its hidden doors on the side and front.

Taylor House is at 208 North Main Street at the intersection with Baker Street, across from the Stevenson Methodist Church in Berlin. The house is open Monday, Wednesday, Friday, and Saturday, mid-May through September from 1:00 to 4:00 P.M. and for special events, such as concerts. Call (410) 641–1019. There is no admission charge.

In the middle of the historic district is the ◆ **Atlantic Hotel,** a faithfully restored 1895 Victorian hostelry that was rescued from the depths of distress to become this showpiece, named to the National Register of Historic Places in 1980.

Each of the sixteen guest rooms (each with private bath) is beautifully furnished with antiques and is unique in its decor. Rich green and burgundy, delicate rose and aqua, deep mahogany tones, tassels, braid, lace, and crochet help transport you to a gentler time and quieter pace. A parlor—for reading, letter writing, or conversation—is on the second floor. If you must have a television in your room, the hotel staff is quite willing to provide one for you.

Continental breakfast is provided. The dinner menu changes periodically to reflect seasonal availabilities, but you might find lobster sauté, stuffed scallops, sole paupiettes, a seafood sampler, or selections "from the land." One interesting offering, either as an appetizer or as part of the sampler, is the coconut shrimp, which is jumbo shrimp dredged in coconut, pan-fried golden brown, and finished with a sweet pepper and mango chutney. Stephen Jacques is general manager and chef, and you should not be surprised if he comes to your table to personally tell you what is on the menu for the day.

The Atlantic Hotel Inn and Restaurant is located at 2 North Main Street, Berlin 21811. Call (410) 641–3589 for information or reservations.

Seven miles east of Berlin is ◆ **Assateague Island National Seashore,** which is reached by Route 611. Nearly two million people visit this seashore annually. A two-room visitor center is open for interpretive classes and exhibits, which include a small "touch tank" of marine life. During a visit here you can take a guided walk; view a demonstration on how to catch blue crabs, clams, and ribbed mussels (mighty tasty steamed or sautéed in butter); or join a naturalist at the Old Ferry Landing to explore the ¾-mile width of Assateague Island. You will travel by foot and bike or car from the salt marsh to the pounding surf, discovering relationships between the various barrier island life zones. The famed Chincoteague ponies can be seen on Assateague, for two herds of the wild ponies make their home here. The herds are separated by a fence at the Maryland-Virginia state line. Managed by the National Park Service on the Maryland side, horses are often seen around roads and campgrounds. The horses sold at auction every July are on the Virginia side. No road connects the two states within the park.

Supposedly, the horses are descended from domesticated stock that grazed on the island as early as the seventeenth century; Eastern Shore planters put them here to avoid mainland taxes and fencing requirements. Smaller than horses, these shaggy, sturdy ponies are well adapted to their harsh seashore environment. Marsh and dune grasses supply the bulk of their food, and they obtain water from freshwater impoundments or natural ponds.

Although they appear tame, they are unpredictable and can inflict serious wounds by kicking and biting. The Park Service strongly recommends that you do not pet or feed the ponies.

You may find great blue herons, snowy egrets, dungins, American widgeons, black-crowned night herons, peregrine falcons, and numerous other birds on the Maryland side, but they are more easily seen on the Virginia side.

Legend has it that Edward Teach (Blackbeard the Pirate) kept one of his fourteen wives, a base of operations, and buried treasure on Assateague. The visitor center is open daily from 8:30 A.M. to 5:00 P.M. For more information call (410) 641–1441.

The VIEWTRAIL 100 signs you will see on secondary state and county roads mark a scenic bicycle trail, which is maintained by the Worcester 4-H Older Youth. You can join the trail in Berlin as it sweeps down to Pocomoke City, past the access to Furnace Town, Nassawango Creek Cypress Swamp, Milburn Landing on the north bank of the Pocomoke River, Mt. Zion One-Room School Museum, and many other interesting attractions. The **Pocomoke River** is the northernmost swamp river on the East Coast, and along its banks are cypress trees (used to make our country's first ships) and Spanish moss. Here you can see eagles, egrets, hawks, and vultures as well.

Another trail, the **Beach to Bay Indian Trail,** is a self-guided driving one that goes from Crisfield on the Chesapeake

Atlantic Hotel

Bay in Somerset County up to Princess Anne, Pocomoke City, Snow Hill, Berlin, and Ocean City. It was opened in the spring of 1988 and is jointly sponsored by Somerset and Worcester Tourism, Ocean City, the State of Maryland, and the departments of Transportation, Natural Resources, and Housing and Community Development. For more Maryland bike trail information, call (410) 333–1663. For travel information about Ocean City, call (800) 62-OCEAN.

A carved-wood relief sculpture in polychrome, called The Power of Communication, hangs over the postmaster's door in the ◆ **Pocomoke City Post Office.** Perna Krick of Baltimore executed the commission in 1940. The figure of an Indian with an airplane reflects the history of the area, from Indian tradition to the development of communication, from primitive methods to present-day service.

Ms. Krick was born in Ohio in 1909 and attended the Dayton Art Institute. She studied under J. Maxwell Miller at the Rinehard School of Sculpture in Baltimore, receiving two European traveling scholarships. By the time she received this commission from the Federal Works Agency, she had exhibited at the Baltimore Art Museum, the Pennsylvania Academy of Fine Arts, and the Architectural League in New York.

One of the traditional sights around Ocean City is the airplanes flying banners about 200 feet above sea level. Robert Bunting of Berlin bought a small crop duster in 1982 and started ❖**airplane advertising** by flying up and down the beach with banner messages. The business is so popular that a half-dozen banner bearing, single-engine aircraft are used for this kind of advertising.

Each banner must have forty or fewer letters. Some carry marriage proposals; others tell you about the newest restaurant in town. If you would like to have one carry your message for the world to see while the plane flies "low and slow," it will cost between $50 and $160 per banner. If you go watch the ground crew rig the planes, you will see them set the banner between two upright poles that are 6 feet apart. (It is said that if the ground crew is feeling prankish, they will close the poles only 2 feet apart.) Then the plane flies about eighty-five miles per hour to pick up the banner. Usually the pilot makes it on the first trip, but it has taken as many as six tries to hook a banner. You are looking at some first-class flying.

Between Memorial Day and Labor Day, each pilot logs about 500 hours, flying from 10:00 A.M. to 4:00 P.M., seven days a week, and together the pilots can fly as many as 110 banners in one day, although the average is about forty-five to fifty.

Ocean City is a family-oriented town on the ocean. It lies 7 miles north of Berlin. Thousands of college kids ("June bugs") come here every summer to work and vacation. There is plenty to do, from kite flying (probably my favorite activity), to boating, fishing, golfing, and checking to make sure the draft beer is kept at the right temperature.

As with any resort, there are dozens (if not hundreds) of restaurants, eateries, bars, and food stands along the 3-mile boardwalk, and you have to try some of the famous saltwater taffy and Thrasher's french fries with vinegar.

The Ocean City restaurant that has to be a first on anyone's list is ❖ **Phillips Crab House.** Eating at this restaurant, which was started by Shirley and Brice Phillips from Hooper's Island on Chesapeake Bay, has been an Ocean City ritual since 1956. The two of them have become such an institution and such an integral part of their community that they were honored in 1989 by the Ocean City Good Will Ambassadors Grand Ball. Phillips has branched out with seven locations, among them a hotel and eateries in Baltimore's Harborplace, Washington, D.C., and Norfolk.

But the Ocean City location is the one to visit. It was a shingle-covered shack in the boonies when it opened. Now it is in the middle of everything that is happening and can seat 1,400 diners at one time. Despite its size, you will have to arrive early or plan to wait awhile because there is always a line for dinner. This is where you come to eat crabs, piled in mounds on broad sheets of paper that cover tables that once held sewing machines. And if steamed crabs, spiced shrimp, and crab cakes don't appeal to you, there is always fried chicken, Virginia baked ham served with corn on the cob, watermelon, and cole slaw. A children's menu is also available.

Phillips Crab House is at Twenty-first Street and Philadelphia Avenue, Ocean City 21842. For information call (410) 289–6821.

Those of you who served aboard the USS *324,* a World War II submarine that was built in 1944 and saw battle in the Java and South China seas, will find her serving a new function as a reef off Ocean City. The *Blenny* was scuttled in 1989 about 15 miles offshore. It acts as a base for algae and soft coral growth, which will attract small fish and then larger fish, fishermen, and divers.

Ocean City is not just for summer fun. It is a year-round community that sponsors a great number of activities during the winter season, including workshops, entertainment, an annual Christmas parade, a traditional lighting and trimming of a 30-foot tree on the beach, the putting up of Christmas decorations throughout the town (call 800–62–OCEAN for details), and numerous other events. A brochure about Christmas in Ocean City (as well as Berlin, Snow Hill, and Pocomoke) is available from the Ocean City Public Relations Office, P.O. Box 158, Ocean

City 21842. You can call the office at (410) 289–2800.

For additional information on Worcester County, contact the Maryland Lower Shore Tourist Information Center (U.S. Route 13 North, 144 Ocean Highway, Pocomoke City 21851; 410–957–2484) or Worcester County Tourism (P.O. Box 208, Snow Hill 21863; 800–852–0335).

DELAWARE

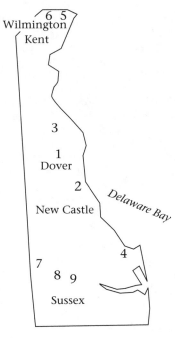

Wilmington
Kent

3

1
Dover

2

New Castle

Delaware Bay

7

8 9

4

Sussex

1. Delaware Agricultural Museum and Village
2. Dover Air Force Base
3. Bombay Hook National Wildlife Refuge
4. Zwaanendael Museum
5. Brandywine Art Museum
6. Hagley Museum
7. *Woodland Ferry*
8. Sweet potato houses
9. Trap Pond State Park

DELAWARE

KENT COUNTY

Kent, the middle of the three Delaware counties, has Dover as its focus. This is the home of the Dover Air Force Base and some Amish families (with their attendant farmers' markets and horse-drawn buggies); it is also the county seat. It's a hubbub of activity and constant change. Here you'll also find such unusually named places as Slaughter Beach, Seven Hickories, Dutch Neck Cross-roads, and Little Heaven.

There are a few intriguing museums, the Delaware Agricultural Museum and Village and the Dover Air Force Base Museum, but Kent County is balanced with an abundance of protected open spaces where you can explore what nature has left for you and the people of Delaware have kept protected for you. Some of the information presented here is thumbnail in nature because it's easy to find your way around such places as Dover; other areas are a little more difficult to uncover and receive a little bit more attention.

The **State House** in Dover is the second-oldest continuously used statehouse (Annapolis, Maryland, is first), and this restored 1792 structure has period furnishings and an exhibit of artifacts and historical items. Guided tours start from the Delaware Visitor Center and Sewell C. Biggs Museum of American Art, which is located behind the statehouse. (Biggs, from the Odessa area, collected art from the eighteenth century to modern times and donated it to this museum, which is named in his honor.) The State House is located at South State Street, on the east side of the green. The entrance is at 406 Federal Street. There is no admission charge, and it is open Tuesday through Saturday from 10:00 A.M. to 4:30 P.M.. and Sunday from 1:30 to 4:30 P.M. Call (302) 739–4266.

If you're in the State House, then you're in the **Capital Green,** which is lined with historic buildings and is the very ground upon which the United States Constitution received its first signature in 1787. If you're taking a guided tour, be sure to ask your leader about the woman who sent poisoned candy to her lover's family, resulting in the death of at least one person. This isn't a modern revenge happening; it took place in the 1890s.

At the **Hall of Records,** near Legislative Hall, is the public archives for the state. This is where you can find the original 1682 charter of King Charles II and William Penn's order for the platting of Dover. The Hall of Records is at Legislative Avenue and Duke of York Street; no charge. It's open Monday through Friday from 8:30 A.M. to 4:15 P.M. Closed on holidays. Call (302) 739–5314.

The ◆ **Delaware Agricultural Museum and Village** covers the agrarian background and heritage of Delaware, with dairy and poultry farming objects, horse-drawn equipment, and tractors from 1670 through the 1950s. There's a barbershop, farmhouse, general store, one-room schoolhouse, sawmill, train station, and blacksmith and wheelwright shops, all representing structures from the Civil War to the turn of this century.

The museum and village are about 2 miles north of Dover, at the junction of US Routes 13 and 13 Alt. It's open Tuesday through Saturday 10:00 A.M. to 4:00 P.M. and Sunday 1:00 to 4:00 P.M. from April through December. The rest of the year, it's open from 10:00 A.M. to 4:00 P.M. It's closed on holidays. Call (302) 734–1618.

For those who like aviation, one of the more exciting places to visit is the ◆ **Dover Air Force Base,** particularly during the open house dates. That's when you'll see dozens of C5As, the military equivalent of the 747. (The plane is big enough to hold several football fields.) Also on display at the base museum is a collection of vintage planes from 1941, including a C-47 Gooney Bird and a B-17G. Other World War II artifacts also are on display. The museum is open Monday through Saturday 9:00 A.M. to 3:00 P.M. but is closed on holidays. There is no admission charge. Dover Air Force Base is on US Route 113, 2 miles south of Dover. Call (302) 677–5938.

Guided tours are offered at the **John Dickinson Plantation,** the boyhood home of John Dickinson who in 1778 drafted the Articles of Confederation. His 1740s brick home and the reconstructed outbuildings are typical of the eighteenth-century plantation architecture and lifestyle. From March through December, it is open Tuesday through Saturday 10:00 A.M. to 3:30 P.M. and Sunday 1:30 to 4:30 P.M. It is closed on holidays. There is no admission charge. The John Dickinson Plantation is on Kitts Hammock Road. Call (302) 739–3277.

Just southeast of Dover, in Magnolia, is the "town sign" that states: THIS IS MAGNOLIA, THE CENTER OF THE UNIVERSE, AROUND WHICH THE WORLD REVOLVES. Magnolia is noted as being one of those little peninsula towns that has not lost its personality in this modern age. The house you'll be looking at when you see this sign is the John B. Lindale House, a Victorian with really neat twin towers. It is a private residence, but you can still admire it.

In Leipsic is an area that grew from the fur trapping and shipping trades of the early nineteenth century. You'll enjoy a visit here if you stop by the ◆ **Bombay Hook National Wildlife Refuge,** where you're sure to spot plenty of ducks, geese, and shorebirds during migrating season (more than one and one-half million shorebirds traverse Delaware in the annual migration in late May and early June), and other wildlife all year-long. You can drive along the 12-mile loop or hike on the nature trails and climb the observation towers for a panoramic view. The refuge is open daily from dawn to dusk, and a visitor center is open daily during the summer and on weekdays during the winter. The admission to the refuge is $4.00 per private vehicle; (302) 653–6872.

Another tribute to agriculture can be found in Harrington at the **Messick Agricultural Museum,** with its extensive display of farm implements of the early twentieth century. You'll see automobiles, a covered wagon, various engines, horse-drawn plows and vehicles, tools, tractors, and trucks. There's also an early twentieth-century kitchen and smokehouse. There are a number of annual events in Harrington, including the Crab Feast in late August, the Heritage Day in late September, and the Delaware State Fair in late July. This is a real old-fashioned state fair that still has strong agricultural roots and has not been "citified."

The town of Smyrna is pretty small but it is growing. At the moment there's no department store, and there are a few other "big town" conveniences that are missing. But it more than makes up for what it lacks in charm. Actually, Smyrna is a historic town that straddles the two counties of New Castle and Kent. The line of demarcation is Duck Creek, located on the north side of the town. On the south side, Lake Como (with a freshwater beach) is a beautiful, small lake surrounded by houses with well-manicured yards and the Delaware Home & Hospital. As one local said, "If I focus, I can see children playing with buckets and shovels in the sand, moms and dads and older kids in stripped woolen swimwear walking on the beach, swimming in the cool waters and diving off the end of the pier."

In town are two eateries that exude hometown goodness. They are the locally well-known **Smyrna Diner,** on DuPont Boulevard, (302) 653–9980, and **The Wayside Inn,** on Route 13, (302) 653–8047.

The accurately self-proclaimed **Boondocks** restaurant receives high marks for seafood and crabs—as well as for the drive out there. It's on Bayview Road; (302) 653–6962.

A must-stop is at Lewes, the Delaware side of the Lewes–Cape May, New Jersey ferry. The hour-plus ride at about $18 a car is a great way to avoid driving up the New Jersey Turnpike and then down to the beach towns of southern New Jersey or Atlantic City. (Call 302–645–6313 or 800–64–FERRY.) But there are other reasons to come to Lewes.

You can't miss the ◆**Zwaanendael Museum** (Valley of the Swans), a Dutch Renaissance building that is an adaptation of the town hall at Hoorn in the Netherlands. No, it wasn't brought over stone by stone and it wasn't built three centuries ago. Instead, it was built in 1931 (the tricentennial anniversary of the founding of Lewes). Inside are exhibits of historic military and maritime artifacts from 1631 to the War of 1812. Located on Savannah Road and King's Highway, it is open Tuesday through Saturday 10:00 A.M. to 4:30 P.M. and Sunday 1:30 to 4:30 P.M. It is closed on holidays. There is no admission charge. Call (302) 645–9418.

Also to be seen, depending on whether you want nature or history, are the **Prime Hook National Wildlife Refuge,** (302) 684–8419, and the **Seaside Nature Center,** (302) 645–6852. At the **Lewes Historical Society Complex** is a furnished country store from the early years of this century, the 1798 Burton-Ingram House with period Chippendale and Empire antiques, and other historic buildings. For curiosity's sake, stop by the Cannonball House on Front Street to see a cannonball in the foundation of the building, a souvenir of the War of 1812.

Zwaanendael Museum

And should you be in the area on the first Saturday of November, you should stop by the Eagle Crest Aerodrome to witness the Punkin Chunkin' contest. It's just what it sounds, a contest to see who can hurl pumpkins the farthest distance by the use of catapults and other odd contraptions.

For information contact Lewes Chamber of Commerce and Visitor's Bureau at 120 Kings Highway, Lewes 19958; (302) 645–8073.

For additional information contact the Kent County Tourism Corporation, 9 East Lockerman Street, Box 576, Dover 19903, (302) 734–1736, or the Delaware Tourism Office, 99 Kings Highway, Box 1401, Dover 19903, (302) 734–1736.

NEW CASTLE COUNTY

Wilmington, the largest city in Delaware, was laid out in 1731 by Quakers and was an important shipping center. Early in the 1800s, Eleuthère Irenée du Pont and his two sons moved into the area and seeing the abundant waterpower potential, started their gunpowder business. Their influence on the development of the city and surrounding area can not be overstated. Eventually the DuPonts would be responsible for building public schools and creating some of the most incredible museums and museum settings.

Draped on either side of the Brandywine Creek that runs from the heart of Wilmington are Brandywine, Alapocas, and Rockford parks. **Brandywine Park** was designed by Frederick Law Olmstead, creator of New York City's Central Park and the National Zoo in Washington, D.C. There's a playground here, a zoo, and the Josephine Garden with its Japanese cherry trees.

A little farther north is the ◆ **Brandywine Art Museum,** with one of the country's most important assemblages of English pre-Raphaelite paintings in the Bancroft collection. American artists also are represented, and a hands-on section is great for children to learn about art. Located at 2301 Kentmere Parkway, the museum is open Tuesday through Saturday 10:00 A.M. to 5:00 P.M. and Sunday noon to 5:00 P.M. The museum is closed on New Year's, Thanksgiving, and Christmas days. The admission for adults is $5.00, seniors over 60, $3.00, and students with identification, $2.50. Call (302) 571–9590.

There are other special places to visit and the ◆ **Hagley Museum** is one of them. Set on 240 landscaped acres at the original DuPont mills, there are numerous exhibits showing the maturation of this country's economic growth. When you consider how explosive gunpowder is, you can look at the architecture and design of the mills with great appreciation. The three side walls farthest from the water were made of heavy stone. The side wall along the creek was made of wood. When the inevitable explosion took place, it would blow out the less-sturdy wooden wall into the creek. This prevented the force of the explosion blowing out walls that would have otherwise damaged other buildings nearby.

The Hagley is open daily 9:30 A.M. to 4:30 P.M. from mid-March to December 31, and weekends 9:30 A.M. to 4:30 P.M. the rest of the year. The Hagley is closed Thanksgiving, Christmas, and New Year's Eve days. Admission is $9.75 for adults, $7.50 for seniors and students, and $3.50 for children. A family rate is available at $26.50. Call (302) 658–2400.

Other highlights of the Wilmington area are Longwood Gardens, Old Swedes Church, Nemours Mansion and gardens, and, most definitely, the Winterthur Museum. A little north of Wilmington is the anomaly of modern government known as **Arden.** It was one of three towns (along with Ardentown and Ardencroft that would come later) created under the principles conceived by Philadelphia-born economist Henry George and his Theory of Single Tax. Born in 1839, George proposed that land only should be taxed, thereby creating the concept of the "single tax." Thus, in 1895, a group of single taxers from Philadelphia invaded Delaware with their political evangelism.

Frank Stephens, a Philadelphia sculptor, with the help of architect Will Price and soap manufacturer Joseph Fels, acquired a Brandywine hundred farm of 160 acres and started the village of Arden. It continues to this day as a single tax entity. Utopian in nature, the community also incorporated the artistic ideas of William Morris and the Arts and Crafts Movement, the Garden Cities planning ideas of Ebenezer Howard, and some social theories of Petr Alekseevich Kropotkin (1842–1921).

Many of the homes are tiny, for they were summer places, but there definitely is a mix of new and old, fancy and ramshackle, set on varying locations on varying-sized lots. The three villages are surrounded by woodlands, including the **Naaman's Creek** natural area, designated as one of "Delaware's Outstanding Natural Areas." There are two things that drive the residents of Arden: the Arden Club and the Arden Community Recreation Association. Music, dance, theater, visual arts, and such crafts as pottery and ironwork are still highly valued in the three Ardens. There is not much for the tourist to "see" in the way of historic buildings or museums, so you have to look at their activities calendar, scheduling your visit for the contra dancing/square dancing every month, the Arden Fair (the Saturday before Labor Day), the Shakespearean productions (*Twelfth Night* and *Macbeth* were presented in 1996) in the little (130-seat) outdoor theater on the Arden Green, and the Candlelight Music Dinner Theater in Ardentown that has shows throughout the year. Call (302) 475–2313 for information.

Old New Castle is filled with Colonial-era homes and buildings that the Rockefeller Foundation initially wanted to restore as a living museum of Colonial America. However, the locals raised such a fuss that the Rockefellers went to Williamsburg, Virginia, instead. Rather than reconstructing the history represented at Williamsburg, New Castle exudes the past from every brick and slather of mortar. It was here that William Penn set foot in North America for the first time. From those Quaker beginnings, the town became a trade center through shipping. A disastrous fire leveled the business area in 1824, but the town was restored when the railroad came through less than a decade later. Then the railroad was re-routed into Wilmington and the town has sat there ever since.

Among the houses that are open for your inspection and journey into the past are the Amstel House, the Dutch House, and the George Read II House and garden. You can also tour the restored Court House, or just spend a lazy afternoon on the green.

The **Amstel House** dates from the 1730s and was the home of Colonial Governor Nicholas Van Dyke. The furnishings show how life was during the Colonial period. It's at Fourth and Delaware streets; (302) 322–2794.

In the **Dutch House** you are touring what is thought to be the oldest brick house in Delaware. Constructed in the late seventeenth century, it has been restored and contains wonderful decorative arts and historical items. It's located at 32 East Third Street; (302) 322–2794.

Both the Amstel and Dutch houses are open from March through December, Tuesday through Saturday 11:00 A.M. to 4:00 P.M. and Sunday 1:00 to 4:00 P.M. They're open on weekends the rest of the year but closed on holidays. Admission to each is $2.00 for adults and $1.00 for children under 12, or you can get a combination ticket for $3.50 for adults and $1.50 for children.

George Read was one of the signers of the Declaration of Independence, and his son's home, called the **George Read II House,** was built over a seven-year period starting in 1797. It's a superb illustration of Federal-style architecture and you'll note the carved woodwork, fanlights, silver door hardware, and period furnishings. A Philadelphia-style adaptation of a Victorian garden decorates the side and back yards. You have a choice of touring this home on your own or calling for an appointment for a guided tour. If you have the time, I recommend the latter. From March through December the George Read II House, at 42 The Strand, is open Tuesday through Saturday 10:00 A.M. to 4:00 P.M.

and Sunday noon to 4:00 P.M. It's open on weekends in the winter, but closed on holidays. The admission is $4.00 for adults, $3.50 for seniors and children 13 to 21, and $2.00 for children 6 to 12. Call (302) 322–8411.

Surely you've noted that the top of the Delaware border, where it meets Pennsylvania, is the arc of a circle. The spire at the top of the New Castle Court House is the center point of the 12-mile radius that marks that arc. Now restored to its 1804 appearance, flags of the Netherlands, Sweden, Great Britain, and the United States represent the various governments that have had jurisdiction over New Castle. Located at 211 Delaware Street, between Market and Third streets, it's open Tuesday through Saturday 10:00 A.M. to 3:30 P.M. and Sunday 1:30 to 4:30 P.M.; closed on state holidays. There is no admission charge. Call (302) 323–4453 or (800) 441–8846.

If there's time, stop by the Old Library Museum (40 East Third Street), the Old Presbyterian Church, and the Original Ticket Office. Then reward yourself with a picnic stop at the green. Located on Delaware Street, between Third and Market streets, it was laid out by Peter Stuyvesant in 1655.

Another delightful little town is Hockessin, just outside of Wilmington. As noted in the Delaware part of the introduction, one of the pleasures of the DelMarVa is the chance to pick up a Nancy Sawin book; she's done at least eleven including *Delaware Sketchbook*, *Backroading Through Cecil (MD) County*, *Between the Bays* (Delaware and Chesapeake), and even one on outhouses entitled *Privy to the Council Seats of Yore*, with sketches of a variety of "necessary" buildings from lean-to to Alpine chalet to one that was fenced and shingled to one that had four columns on its porch. One of my great delights is driving through the state and trying to spot the object Ms. Sawin has drawn.

Sawin was born in Wilmington in 1917, and when she retired in 1974 from a life in education, she started writing and illustrating books on local history. Her home is adjacent to Sandford School, where she had been teacher, coach, and headmistress. She refers to her home as a "semimuseum of early 'Americana'" and some of the items therein are for sale. Visitors are welcome, but please call first. Nancy C. Sawin, 147 Sawin Lane, Hockessin; (302) 239–2416.

As you're driving around this area you may want to try the

Back Burner restaurant. They have delicious seafood and meat entrées and friendly and attentive service. It's a small space, and people from Wilmington make a special drive "to the country" for the food. The Back Burner is at 425 Old Lancaster Pike; (302) 239–2314. The old post office across the street from the Back Burner is Alleman & Co., now a new "antiques" store. Locals who jog through Hockessin know there's an old gardener on Evanson Road who has nailed a basket to a tree on his property that is right next to the road. Every summer day there are fresh tomatoes, zucchini, chilis, and various other delights for any passersby to grab.

For additional information write to the Wilmington Convention and Visitors Bureau, 1300 Market Street, Suite 504, Wilmington 19801 or call (302) 652–4088. You can also contact the New Castle Visitors Bureau, Box 465, New Castle 19720; (302) 322–8411 or (800) 748–1550.

SUSSEX COUNTY

As one might expect, the town of **Laurel** (originally Laureltown) was so-named because of the abundance of laurel bushes growing along Broad Creek. Settled in 1802, the town was the largest in Sussex County by 1859 and was once a thriving shipping center and port town. With more than 800 buildings on the National Register of Historic Places, it is the largest designated historic district in the state of Delaware. Many properties were destroyed in the "Great Fire" of 1899, but others survived. Pick up a "Walking Tour of Historic Laurel" brochure from the historical society to see some of the fascinating moments from the past.

As small as Bethel and the area around it is, there are enough people to see and talk to—and even things to do and learn—that you might find ways to spend an entire day there—even a lifetime. Start with the Laurel-Woodland ferry, more commonly called the ◆ *Woodland Ferry,* that crosses the Nanticoke River just as boats have done since 1793. It's the last free and last river ferry in Delaware. The *Virginia C.*, apparently named for the wife of a former captain, is a diesel-powered cable-guided ferry that can carry three cars on its six-minute ride across the river. Operated from sunup to sundown by captains John Illiston and John and Bonnie Maull, the ferry may make up to three hundred trips on a busy day, saving its passengers a road trip of nearly 20 miles. Signs on Route 78 in Laurel and Reliance, Route 490 south of Blades, and Route 80 at Seaford indicate if the ferry is running. Call (302) 629–7742.

On the western side of the Nanticoke is the town of Woodland, with a population of about 100 people. As the Nanticoke is known for its shad and Woodland is known for its hospitality, you might want to schedule your visit for the annual spring shad supper held by the women of the Woodland Methodist Church.

While in Bethel you'll want to stop by Jeff Hastings's farm market to buy some fresh produce. He's been known to have some spectacular seedless watermelon. And just past his place is the Bethel Store. They have soft ice cream that's pretty good, costs less than a dollar for a cone, and is made with real milk, not the skimpy, thin, fat-free stuff. You have to time your tastes to the days of the week. According to Mark Shaver (who's been connected with this family store for sixteen years), they used to have only vanilla. Then some customers started requesting chocolate, so he did that one day a week. Then they started clamoring for more. So now it's chocolate three days a week, on Monday, Wednesday, and Friday. The rest of the week it's vanilla. Shaver says they're too poor to afford two machines to make both every day. I would add that there isn't enough room in the store for two machines.

Across the street is the post office, where Bettie Stoakley has been postmaster for the past sixteen years, serving 120 families. Yes, it's on old house, and as you go in you'll notice the bottom tread and riser of some stairs that used to go up to a second floor. Stoakley says it's been that way since before she arrived.

In Laurel, as well as Milton, Ridgeville, and Milford, and other places, you'll see murals by Jack Lewis, a graduate of Rutgers with a master's degree in education. You'll find them on exterior walls, in banks, in the family court in Georgetown, and even in a prison. He's been teaching art in the state for thirty years, and he participated in a Fulbright Scholarship exchange program. Basically, Lewis says, he's a watercolorist, and murals are not his chief interest. Fortunately, he has dabbled in the area murals, for our enjoyment. Call (302) 337–8840 for more information

The Laurel area is noted for at least one other bit of historical trivia. On June 21, 1904, some signals were crossed and the schooner, *Golden Gate*, traveling down the nearby Broad Creek, was struck by a mail train. Luckily the train engine automatically uncoupled, so the rest of the train didn't fall into the creek. This may be the only occurrence of a train and sailing ship colliding.

The **Spring Garden Bed & Breakfast,** with Gwen or (Gwenie) North as your hostess, is an excellent place to use as a base for your local explorations. Her half-Victorian and half-Colonial home has been lovingly restored and is among the buildings on the National Register of Historic Places. North's family has been in this area since the seventeenth century, and Gwen has her finger on about as much history as you'll want. There are two bedrooms downstairs and four upstairs. She was the first winner of the Governor's State Tourism Award. The gardens are particularly inviting, and Gwen grows enough herbs to offer some to her guests so they'll remember her even when they return home. Call Spring Garden at (302) 875–7015.

Talk to Gwen about the ❖ **sweet potato houses,** and if you're really interested, she'll tell you where to see some, or she'll

Sweet potato houses

call Kendall Jones for you and he'll take you on a tour. In a nut-shell, or in a potato skin if you will, the life of a sweet potato is not easy. The seeds first must be started indoors in February. Then they must be transplanted to warm beds, then to the out-doors, and then harvested and dried. Sweet potatoes apparently are horrible if eaten when freshly harvested. They'll keep all win-ter if they're stored in a constant 50-degree temperature. Ergo, these buildings were constructed to hold the very productive sweet potato cash crop.

The buildings are usually two to three stories tall and are long and relatively narrow. They include three or more layers of wood siding. On the exterior is a horizontal layer, followed by a diago-nal layer in the center, and a vertical layer on the inside. All this helped to insulate the building, and sometimes a form of tar paper or sawdust was used between the layers to further insulate it. Inside are a series of bins, about 3 feet by 9 feet, where the potatoes were stored. Sometimes access to the bins was from a central aisle, sometimes from a perimeter walkway. A stove at one end had to be tended morning and night once the first frost had set in. The second and third floors did not butt against the walls; this helped ventilation and ensured an even distribution of the heat to the upper and lower floors.

A blight hit the extremely labor-intensive crop in the 1940s and destroyed the industry. Now, some of the sweet potato or potato houses have been converted into office or living space.

If you'd like to just drive by one, there's an excellent example across from the old Christ Church on Route 24, about a mile east of Route 13 just south of the intersection with Route 9. It's slightly different from most sweet potato houses because of the number of window it has, but you'll get the idea.

Gwen's Spring Garden B & B is one of three (soon to be more) on a **Bike & Bed** program. A second is **Eli's Country Inn** near Greenwood. This is a painstakingly renovated farmhouse in the country, where you literally can hear the quiet. Seven sisters, Cora Tennefloss, Betty Sharp, Anna, Olive, Margaret, Sarah, and Wanda, more or less run this home where they spent their child-hood. Your trip will be complete when you meet Cora's husband, Tom. The first thing he'll ask is, "Did you graduate high school?" He'll follow this with, "What does Y-E-S spell?" (I won't spoil the rest of his routine, but if you know the secret to his "yip stick" or learn it from him somehow, please let me know.) Two rooms downstairs are accessible, and there is plenty of room on the porches and decks for sitting around in the afternoon if you don't want to go do something. With seventy-eight-plus acres, planted with soybeans, fresh fruits, and vegetables, you can also do some gardening if you want. The organ is original, and the home has a vacuum cleaner motor powering it. Eli's Country Inn is on Route 36, Greenwood 19950-0779. Call (302) 349–4265, (800) 594–0048, or (302) 349–9340.

This four-day/three-night inn-to-inn bike touring experience averages 30–45 miles of back roads pedaling. You'll go through small towns and past so many antiques stores that you wish you were in a car so you could cart home some of those treasures, or be glad you're on a bike and can't buy anything. You'll go past a bison farm. The package includes three nights' accommodation, hotel tax, luggage transportation from inn to inn, three breakfasts and three dinners, snacks at each inn on arrival, detailed maps with points of interest, and secure bike storage. Call Ambassador Travel at (800) 845–9939. As of this writing, the cost is $300, p.p./d.o. for weeknights. Weekend rates are slightly higher. Extra nights are available upon request.

Do be warned that the local Greenwood police like to park at the intersection of Route US 13 and State Route 16, just waiting for out-of-state drivers to speed by.

Britt's Dutch Inn, established in 1948, is one of those "down-home" community restaurants that's open 6:00 A.M. to 9:00 P.M. daily and features great seafood and delicious desserts. As of this writing, you could get an Eastern Shore platter with ham, chicken salad, and a crab cake for $10.50, and it was one of the more expensive items on the menu. It came with two vegetables, rolls, and butter. Forget all the lectures about healthy fat-free and no-taste food; this is about as good a place as any to try the local delicacy called slippery dumplings. It also seems that this might be the place to stop in if you want to know what's going on in this town. Britt's Dutch Inn is located on South Central Avenue; (302) 875–7158.

There's no telling where you might think you are when you go through ◆ **Trap Pond State Park.** This 2,000-plus acre park was once part of the large freshwater swampland of southwestern Sussex County. The pond was created in the early 1800s for a sawmill that processed the bald cypress trees from the area. In the 1930s the federal government purchased the area and the Civilian Conservation Corps developed the recreation site. Within the park are bald cypress trees (the northernmost stand in the United States), wetlands, wildflowers, wildlife, a nature preserve, a picnic area, a playground, a primitive camping area for youngsters, more than 7 miles of hiking trails, a canoe trail (perhaps the only marked canoe trail on the Eastern Shore), camping, and a rent-a-camp program that lets you rent equipment to see if you like the experience before investing in all the gear. Birders can spy on great blue herons, owls, hummingbirds, robins, mockingbirds, cardinals, finches, warblers, bald eagles, and pileated woodpeckers.

Pets are permitted in some areas of the park, but they must be kept on a leash and attended to at all times. Bicycles and horses are permitted on designated trails. Motorboats (electric only) are permitted in some areas of the pond and are limited to a no-wake speed of 5 miles per hour. Rowboats, pedal boats, and canoes may be rented in the summer.

The park is part of a trash-free program, which means you carry out everything you carry in. There is a small entrance fee during the summer and on weekends and holidays in May, September, and October. Call (302) 875–5153 or (302) 875–2392 (campground).

As you drive the 20 miles along the beach, from the Maryland border to Lewes (the first town in the first state), you may notice seven concrete towers rising up about 80 feet. They've been there for a number of years, since the days when German U-boats were a threat to our shores. They belong to the state, but there have been days when people were ready to tear them down. After all, they weren't being used. But there wasn't ever enough money, so they still stood. Now, people (perhaps the same ones) have decided the towers are historic. That means you may climb the 115 steps of the Cape Henlopen State Park tower to the top for a lovely view that stretches from the Rehoboth boardwalk to Gordons Pond, taking in the Atlantic Ocean, Delaware Bay, and the outlying salt marsh. It's open seven days a week during the summer season in good weather. It's open on weekends the rest of the year. The admission price is $2.50 for state residents and $5.00 for out-of-staters. Call (302) 645–8983.

For additional information on touring Delaware, contact one or more of the following offices:

Sussex County Convention and Tourism, Box 240, Georgetown 19947; (302) 856–1818.

Greater Georgetown Chamber of Commerce, Box 1, Georgetown 19947; (302) 856–1544.

Greater Seaford Chamber of Commerce, Box 26, Seaford; (302) 629–9690.

Greater Milford Chamber of Commerce, Box 805, Milford; (302) 422–3344.

Rehoboth Beach–Dewey Beach Chamber of Commerce, Box 216, Rehoboth Beach 19971; (302) 227–2233.

Milton Chamber of Commerce, 104 Federal Street, Milton 19968; (302) 684–2504.

Bethany-Fenwick Chamber of Commerce, Box 1450, Bethany Beach 19971; (302) 645–6838.

INDEX

ABOUT THE AUTHOR

Judy Colbert is a longtime resident of Maryland. An award-winning freelance writer and photographer, Judy's articles and photographs have appeared in such publications as *Washingtonian*, *Maryland*, *AAA World*, *American Health*, *Home & Away*, *Self*, and *Frequent Flyer*. She has appeared on "Good Morning America," and Arthur Frommer's "Almanac of Travel."

Other titles that Judy has authored include *The Spa Guide* and *Virginia: Off the Beaten Path*, both published by The Globe Pequot Press.